THE FAT-FREE
COOKBOOK

THE FAT-FREE COOKBOOK

OVER 50 NUTRITIOUS AND TASTY
FAT-FREE RECIPES, PERFECT
FOR ANY OCCASION

CONSULTANT EDITOR
ANNE SHEASBY

LORENZ BOOKS

This edition first published in 1998 by Lorenz Books
27 West 20th Street
New York, NY 10011

LORENZ BOOKS are available for bulk purchase for sales promotion and for
premium use. For details, write or call the sales director, Lorenz Books,
27 West 20th Street, New York, NY 10011; (800) 354-9657

ISBN 1 85967 670 7

Publisher: Joanna Lorenz
Senior Cookery Editor: Linda Fraser
Editor: Margaret Malone
Designer: Ian Sandom
Nutritional Analysis: Wendy Doyle
Photography: Karl Adamson, Edward Allwright, Steve Baxter, James Duncan,
Amanda Heywood, Don Last, Patrick McLeavey, Michael Michaels,
Thomas Odulate and Peter Reilly
Recipes: Catherine Atkinson, Carla Capalbo, Kit Chan, Roz Denny, Christine
France, Shirley Gill, Christine Ingram, Sue Maggs, Annie Nichols, Maggie
Pannell, Laura Washburn and Stephen Wheeler

Printed and bound in Singapore

3 5 7 9 10 8 6 4

CONTENTS

INTRODUCTION

Cooking and eating good food is one of life's greatest pleasures – and there's nothing wrong with enjoying good food, except that for too long good often meant fatty. Butter, oil, cheese and other fatty foods were considered essential for good cooking. We know now that all this fat – along with too much sugar and salt – has a huge impact on health.

Most of us eat fats in one form or another every day. In fact, we need to consume a small amount of fat to maintain a healthy and balanced diet, but almost everyone can afford to, and should, reduce their fat intake, particularly of saturated fats. Weight for weight, dietary fats supply far more energy than all the other nutrients in our diet. If you eat a diet that is high in fats and don't exercise enough to use up that energy, you will put on weight. By cutting down on fat, you can easily reduce your energy intake without affecting the other essential nutrients. And by choosing the right types of fat, using low fat and fat-free products whenever possible, and making small, simple changes to the way you cook and prepare food, you can reduce your overall fat intake quite dramatically and enjoy a much healthier diet without really noticing any difference.

As you will see, watching your fat intake doesn't have to mean dieting and deprivation. *The Fat-Free Cookbook* opens with an easy-to-follow informative introduction about basic healthy eating guidelines – you'll find out about the five main food groups, and how, by simply choosing a variety of foods from these groups every

day, you can ensure that you are eating all the nutrients you need. One way to enjoy your favorite foods without guilt is to substitute lower fat ingredients for higher fat ones. This book will introduce you to these lower fat ingredients and show you how to use them. There are hints and tips on how to cook with fat-free and low fat ingredients; techniques for using healthy, fat-free fruit purée in place of butter or margarine in all your favorite baking recipes; suggestions for which foods to cut down on and what to try instead; easy ways to reduce fat and saturated fat in your foods; new no fat and low fat cooking techniques and information on the best cookware for fat-free cooking; along with a delicious section on low fat and very low fat snacks.

There are over 50 easy-to-follow recipes for delicious dishes that your whole family can enjoy. Every recipe has been developed to fit into modern nutritional guidelines, and each one has at-a-glance nutritional information so you can instantly check the calories and fat content. The recipes are very low in fat – all contain less than five grams of fat per serving and many contain less than one. The selection of foods included will surprise you: there are barbecues and casseroles, pizza and pastas, tasty sautés and stews, vegetable dishes and vegetarian main courses, fish and seafood dishes galore and delicious breads, cookies and cakes. All without as much fat as traditional recipes, of course, but packed with flavor and vitality.

Fresh vegetables and beans (far left) and fresh fruit (left and above) make ideal choices for fat-free and low fat cooking.

HEALTHY EATING GUIDELINES

A healthy diet is one that provides the body with all the nutrients it needs to be able to grow and repair properly. By eating the right types, balance and proportions of foods, we are more likely to feel healthy, have plenty of energy and a higher resistance to illness that will help protect our body against developing diseases such as heart disease, cancers, bowel disorders and obesity.

By choosing a variety of foods every day, you will ensure that you are supplying your body with all the essential nutrients, including vitamins and minerals, it needs. To get the balance right, it is important to know just how much of each type of food you should be eating.

There are five main food groups (see right), and it is recommended that we eat plenty of fruit, vegetables (at least five portions a day, not including potatoes) and foods such as cereals,

pasta, rice and potatoes; moderate amounts of meat, fish, poultry and dairy products; and only small amounts of foods containing fat or sugar. By choosing a good balance of foods from these groups every day, and choosing lower fat or lower sugar alternatives wherever possible, we will be supplying our bodies with all the nutrients they need for optimum health.

THE ROLE AND IMPORTANCE OF FAT IN OUR DIET

Fats shouldn't be cut out of our diets completely. We need a small amount of fat for general health and well-being – fat is a valuable source of energy, and also helps make food more palatable to eat. However, if you lower the fats, especially saturated fats, in your diet, you will feel healthier; it will help you lose weight and reduce the risk of developing some diseases.

THE FIVE MAIN FOOD GROUPS

● Fruit and vegetables

● Rice, potatoes, bread, pasta and other cereals

● Meat, poultry, fish and alternative proteins

● Milk and other dairy foods

● Foods which contain fat and foods which contain sugar

Aim to limit your daily intake of fats to no more than 30% of total calories. In real terms, this means that for an average intake of 2,000 calories per day, 30% of energy would come from 600 calories. Since each gram of fat provides 9 calories, your total daily intake should be no more than 66.6g fat. Your total intake of saturated fats should be no more than 10% of the total calories.

TYPES OF FAT

All fats in our foods are made up of building blocks of fatty acids and glycerol and their properties vary according to each combination.

There are two types of fat – saturated and unsaturated. The unsaturated group is divided into two types – polyunsaturated and monounsaturated fats.

There is always a combination of each of the three types of fat (saturated, polyunsaturated and monounsaturated fats) in any food, but the amount of each type varies greatly from one food to another.

Left: By choosing a variety of foods from the five main food groups, you will ensure that you are supplying your body with all the nutrients it needs.

SATURATED FATS

All fatty acids are made up of chains of carbon atoms. Each atom has one or more free "bonds" to link with other atoms, and by doing so the fatty acids transport nutrients to cells throughout the body. Without these free "bonds" the atom cannot form any links, that is to say it is completely "saturated." Because of this, the body finds it hard to process the fatty acid into energy, so it simply stores it as fat.

Saturated fats are the fats which you should reduce, as they can increase the level of cholesterol in the blood, which in turn can increase the risk of developing heart disease.

The main sources of saturated fats are animal products, such as meat, and fats, such as butter and lard that are solid at room temperature. However, there are also saturated fats of vegetable origin, notably coconut and palm oils, and some margarines and oils, which are processed by changing some of the unsaturated fatty acids to saturated ones – they are labeled "hydrogenated vegetable oil" and should be avoided.

POLYUNSATURATED FATS

There are two types of polyunsaturated fats, those of vegetable or plant origin (omega 6), such as sunflower oil, soft margarine and seeds, and those from oily fish (omega 3), such as herring, mackerel and sardines. Both fats are usually liquid at room temperature. Small quantities of polyunsaturated fats are essential for good health and are thought to help reduce the level of cholesterol in the blood.

MONOUNSATURATED FATS

Monounsaturated fats are also thought to have the beneficial effect of reducing the blood cholesterol level and this could explain why in some

Above: A selection of foods containing the three main types of fat found in foods.

Mediterranean countries there is such a low incidence of heart disease. Monounsaturated fats are found in foods such as olive oil, rapeseed oil, some nuts such as almonds and hazelnuts, oily fish and avocados.

CUTTING DOWN ON FATS AND SATURATED FATS IN THE DIET

About one quarter of the fat we eat comes from meat and meat products, one-fifth from dairy products and margarine and the rest from breads, biscuits, pastries and other foods. It is easy to cut down on obvious sources of fat in the diet, such as butter, oils, margarine, cream, whole milk and high fat cheese, but we also need to know

about – and watch out for – "hidden" fats. Hidden fats can be found in foods such as cakes, biscuits and nuts. Even lean, trimmed red meats may contain as much as 10% fat.

By being aware of foods which are high in fats and particularly saturated fats, and by making simple changes to your diet, you can reduce the total fat content of your diet quite considerably. Whenever possible, choose reduced fat or low fat alternatives to foods, such as milk, cheese and salad dressings, and fill up on very low fat foods, such as fruit and vegetables, and foods that are high in carbohydrate such as pasta, rice, bread and potatoes.

NATURE'S LOW FAT INGREDIENTS

Cutting down on fat doesn't mean sacrificing taste. It's easy to follow a healthy eating plan without having to forgo all your favorite foods. What is necessary, is to choose ingredients that are naturally lower in fat and prepare them with little – if any – additional fat. This is not as limiting as it sounds, as the following ingredients show.

FRUIT

● *Fresh Fruit* – Vitamin C is found almost exclusively in fruit and vegetables and because this vitamin cannot be stored by the body, levels need to be replenished continually. Fruits can be enjoyed raw or cooked: eat them raw in a salad; poach in fruit juice and serve hot with low fat yogurt or serve chunks on cocktail sticks as mini skewers.

● *Dried Fruit* – A good selection of dried fruit is available including apples, apricots, bananas, currants, figs, kiwi fruit, mangoes, peaches, pears, prunes, pineapple and raisins. Low in fat and high in dietary fiber, dried fruit makes a delicious, healthy snack when you feel the need to nibble. Add to breakfast cereals, muesli or oatmeal and use in cakes, cookies and other dessert recipes.

VEGETABLES

● *Fresh Vegetables* – These play an important part in a healthy, balanced diet. Valuable sources of vitamins and minerals, especially vitamins A, C and E, vegetables also contain lots of dietary fiber. Use frozen produce when fresh is not available – it is perfectly acceptable from a nutritional point of view.

Vegetables are often prepared using high fat methods. Below are just a few examples of everyday vegetables with some tips on how they can be prepared using low fat techniques.
Eggplant– Sprinkle with salt, soak for 30 minutes then rinse to draw out the juices and make them less spongy. Do not fry but brush lightly with oil and broil or blanch.
Mushrooms – Sweat in a little stock rather than butter or use raw in salads. Reconstituted dried mushrooms are excellent for adding an intense flavor to

Above: Look no further than fresh fruit for a delicious and healthy snack.

sauces, rice and pasta dishes.
Onions – An essential flavoring for many savory dishes, sweat in stock or cook slowly with some red wine and herbs, rather than fry in oil.
Potatoes – High in carbohydrate, low in fat and containing some vitamin C and dietary fiber, especially if the skins are left on, potatoes are very valuable in terms of nutrition. Traditionally roasted or fried, try instead boiling, steaming or baking.
Zucchini – Very absorbent, zucchini will soak up fat like a sponge if fried. Instead, cook in a tomato sauce, steam with a sprinkling of fresh herbs or thread chunks onto skewers and grill.

PASTA AND GRAINS

● *Oats and Oatmeal* – Just 2 ounces of oats or oat bran a day, as part of a low fat diet, is known to dramatically reduce blood cholesterol. Oats and oatmeal come in a variety of types including whole oats, steel-cut oats, rolled 'old fashioned' oats, rolled 'quick-cooking' oats and 'instant' oatmeal. Use them in muesli, oatcakes, mixed with flour for breads and rolls and in baked goods. Oats are also a good thickener for soups.

Left: Experiment with the wonderful range of fresh vegetables available today – you can't go wrong!

● *Pasta* – Containing very little fat, pasta is an ideal food on which to base a low fat diet. Pasta, like bread, potatoes, cereal, rice and most fruits, is high in filling "complex" carbohydrate, and when broken down by the body, it allows a steady release of energy to keep us satisfied for a long period of time. A nutritious and satisfying meal can be made simply by combining any pasta with a low fat sauce.

Pasta comes in a wide variety of shapes, colors and flavors. Don't worry if you can't find the exact variety suggested in a recipe, a general rule is that long strands such as spaghetti work best with thinner sauces, while short pasta shapes are good with chunky sauces. Sheets of pasta are ideal for layered dishes, and tiny shapes are added to soups.

● *Rice* – Like pasta, rice makes an ideal, versatile basis for a low fat diet. There are thousands of varieties of rice grown all over the world, with differing flavors and aromas. Choose from long grain rice such as basmati, short grain rice such as arborio and medium grain rice. Brown rice, like all whole-grain cereals, has greater nutritional value, especially fiber.

The simplest way to cook rice is in a large quantity of boiling water, however valuable nutrients will be discarded in the leftover water. Try instead steaming or baking rice, allowing the rice to absorb all the water during the cooking.

BEANS AND LEGUMES

● *Fresh* – There are many varieties of fresh beans and legumes available, including peas, fava beans and wax beans and more unusual ones such as flageolet beans and black-eyed peas.

All are low in fat and are good sources of dietary fiber and contain other nutrients including vitamins and

Above: Nutritious and versatile – pasta, rice, beans and pulses play a key role in a healthy low fat diet.

minerals. Very versatile, they can be used in many dishes including salads, stir-fries, stews, pasta sauces, soups and curries. Some varieties, such as sugar snap peas and snow peas can be eaten either raw in salads or cooked.

● *Canned* – Varieties include black-eyed peas, lima beans, chickpeas, flageolet beans, lentils, peas and red kidney beans. Very nutritious and convenient to use, it is well worth having a few cans in your cupboard.

You can reduce the amount of meat used in a recipe by replacing it with some cooked legumes such as lentils, or try mashed cooked legumes as a good basis for dips.

● *Dried* – When buying, choose legumes that are plump and clear in color and avoid broken, shriveled or dusty beans. They should be stored in a cool, dry place in an airtight container and used within one year.

Most dried legumes need to be soaked in water for a period and then boiled until tender. The older the beans

are, the longer they will take to cook, and salt should be added at the end of the cooking time.

HERBS

● In cooking, herbs are used mainly for their flavoring and seasoning properties, as well as for adding color and texture. By simply adding a single herb or a combination of herbs to food, everyday dishes can be transformed into delicious meals.

Herbs are very low in fat and calories and many, such as parsley, also provide useful vitamins and minerals.

POULTRY AND FISH

● A good source of quality protein, B vitamins and some iron, poultry is low in fat, particularly if the skin is removed. All fish is rich in protein, B vitamins and minerals, but choose white fish for its very low levels of fat. Broil or bake fish in the oven and sprinkle with lemon or lime juice and chopped fresh herbs.

Fat Reducing Tips

There are lots of simple no-fuss ways of reducing the fat in your diet. Just follow the simple "eat less – try instead" suggestions below to discover how easy it is.

● *Eat less* – Butter, margarine and hard fats.
● *Try instead* – Low fat spread or polyunsaturated margarine. If you must use butter or solid margarine, make sure they are softened at room temperature and spread them very thinly. Better still, use low fat spreads such as low fat soft cheese, reduced sugar jellies or marmalades for sandwiches and toast.

● *Eat less* – Fatty meats and products such as meat pâtés, hot pies and sausages.
● *Try instead* – Low fat meats, such as chicken, turkey and venison.
Use only the leanest cuts of such meats as lamb, beef and pork.
Always cut any visible fat and skin from meat before cooking.
Choose reduced fat sausages and meat products and eat fish more often.
Try using low fat protein products such as tofu in place of meat in recipes.
Make gravies using vegetable water or fat-free stock rather than using meat juices.

● *Eat less* – Full fat dairy products such as whole milk, cream, butter, sour cream, whole milk yogurts and hard cheese.
● *Try instead* – Low fat or skim milk and milk products, low fat yogurts, low fat ricotta cheese and low fat soft cheeses, reduced fat hard cheeses such as Cheddar, and reduced fat creams and sour cream.

● *Eat less* – Deep-fried French fries and sautéed potatoes.
● *Try instead* – Fat-free starchy foods such as pasta, couscous and rice. Choose baked or boiled potatoes.

● *Eat less* – Solid cooking fats, such as lard or hard margarine.
● *Try instead* – Polyunsaturated or monounsaturated oils such as olive, sunflower or corn for cooking.

● *Eat less* – Fried foods.
● *Try instead* – Fat-free cooking methods such as broiling, microwaving, steaming or baking whenever possible.
Try cooking in a nonstick wok with only a very small amount of mono- or polyunsaturated oil.
Always roast or broil meat or poultry on a rack.

● *Eat less* – High fat snacks such as potato chips, tortilla chips, fried snacks and pastries, chocolate cakes, muffins, donuts, sweet pastries and cookies – especially avoid the chocolate ones!
● *Try instead* – Low fat and fat-free fresh or dried fruits, breadsticks or vegetable sticks.
Make your own home-baked low fat cakes and baked goods.
If you do buy ready-made cakes and cookies, always choose low fat and reduced fat versions.

● *Eat less* – Rich salad dressings like full fat mayonnaise, Thousand Island dressing or French dressing.
● *Try instead* – Reduced fat or fat-free mayonnaise or dressings. Make salad dressings at home with low fat yogurt or ricotta cheese.

● *Eat less* – Added fat in cooking.
● *Try instead* – To cook with little or no fat. Use heavy or good quality nonstick pans, so that the food doesn't stick.
Try using a small amount of spray oil in cooking to control exactly how much fat you are using.
Use fat-free or low fat ingredients for cooking, such as fruit juice, low fat or fat-free stock, wine or even beer.

FAT-FREE COOKING METHODS

It's very easy to cook without fat – whenever possible, broil, bake, microwave or steam foods without the addition of fat, or try stir-frying without fat – use a little low fat or fat-free stock, wine or fruit juice instead.

● Choosing heavy or good quality cookware, you'll find that the amount of fat needed for cooking foods can be kept to an absolute minimum.

● When making stews or meat sauces such as bolognese, dry fry the meat to brown it and then drain off all the excess fat before adding the other ingredients. If you do need a little fat for cooking, choose an oil that is high in unsaturates such as corn, olive or sunflower oil and always use as little as possible.

● When baking low fat cakes and cookies, use good quality bakeware which doesn't need greasing before use, or use nonstick parchment paper and only lightly grease the tin before lining it.

● Look out for nonstick coated fabric sheet. This re-usable nonstick material is amazingly versatile, it can be cut to size and used to line cake tins, baking sheets or frying pans. Heat resistant up to 550°F and microwave safe, it will last for up to 5 years.

● When baking foods such as chicken or fish, rather than adding a pat of butter, try baking the food in a loosely sealed package of foil or grease-proof paper and adding some wine or fruit juice and herbs or spices before sealing the package.

● When broiling foods, the addition of fat is often unnecessary. If the food shows signs of drying, lightly brush with a small amount of unsaturated oil such as sunflower or corn oil.

Above: Invest in a few of these useful items of cookware for easy fat-free cooking: nonstick cookware and accurate measuring equipment are essential.

● Microwaved foods rarely need the addition of fat, so add herbs or spices for extra flavor and color.

● Steaming or boiling are easy, fat-free ways of cooking many foods, such as vegetables, fish and chicken.

● Try poaching foods, such as chicken, fish and fruit, in stock or syrup – it is another easy, fat-free cooking method.

● Try braising vegetables in the oven in low fat or fat-free stock, wine or simply water with the addition of some herbs.

● Sauté vegetables in low fat or fat-free stock, wine or fruit juice instead of fat or oil.

● Cook fresh vegetables in a covered saucepan over a low heat with only a little boiling water so they cook in their own juices.

● Marinate food such as meat or poultry in mixtures of alcohol, herbs or spices, and soy sauce, vinegar or fruit juice. This will help to tenderize the meat and add flavor, aroma and color and, in addition, the marinade can be used to baste the food while it is cooking.

● When serving vegetables such as boiled potatoes, carrots or peas, resist the temptation to add a pat of butter or margarine. Instead, sprinkle with chopped fresh herbs, such as parsley and cilantro or ground spices, such as ginger.

COOKING WITH LOW FAT OR NON-FAT INGREDIENTS

Nowadays many foods are available in full fat and reduced fat or very low fat forms. In every supermarket you'll find a huge array of low fat dairy products, such as milk, cream, yogurt, hard and soft cheeses and ricotta cheese; reduced fat sweet or chocolate cookies; reduced fat or fat-free salad dressings and mayonnaise; reduced fat chips and snacks; low fat, half-fat or very low fat spreads; as well as such reduced fat ready-made food products as desserts.

Other foods, such as fresh fruit and vegetables, pasta, rice, potatoes and bread, naturally contain very little fat. Some foods, such as soy sauce, wine, cider, sherry, sugar, honey, syrup and jam, contain no fat at all. By combining these and other low fat foods you can create delicious dishes which contain very little fat.

Some low fat or reduced fat ingredients and products work better than others in cooking, but often a simple substitution of one for another will work. The addition of low fat or non-fat ingredients, such as herbs and spices, also add plenty of extra flavor and color to recipes.

LOW FAT SPREADS IN COOKING

There is a huge variety of low fat, reduced fat and half-fat spreads available in our supermarkets, along with some spreads that are very low in fat. Some are suitable for cooking, while others are suitable only for spreading.

Generally speaking, the very low fat spreads with a fat content of around 20% or less have a high water content and so are unsuitable for cooking and are suitable only for spreading.

Low fat or half-fat spreads with a fat content of around 40% are suitable for spreading and can be used for some cooking methods. They are suitable for recipes such as all-in-one cake and biscuit recipes, all-in-one sauce recipes, sautéing vegetables over low heat, choux pastry and some cake frostings.

When using these low fat spreads for cooking, the fat may behave slightly differently to full fat products such as butter or margarine.

With some recipes, the cooked result may be slightly different, but will still be very acceptable. Other recipes will be just as tasty and successful. For example, choux pastry made using half- or low fat spread is often slightly crisper and lighter in texture than traditional choux pastry, and a cheesecake cookie crust made with melted half- or low fat spread combined with crushed cookie crumbs, may be slightly softer in texture and less crispy than a cookie crust made using melted butter.

When heating half- or low fat spreads, never cook them over high heat. Always use a heavy pan over low heat to avoid the product burning, spitting or spoiling, and stir all the time. With all-in-one sauces, the mixture should be whisked continuously over low heat.

Half-fat or low fat spreads are not suitable for shallow or deep-fat frying, pastry making, rich fruit cakes, some cookies, shortcake, clarified butter and preserves such as lemon curd.

Remember that the storage times for recipes made using half- or low fat spreads may be reduced slightly, because of the lower fat content.

Almost all dairy products now come in low fat or reduced fat versions.

Another way to reduce the fat content of recipes, particularly cake recipes is to use a fruit purée in place of all or some of the fat in a recipe.

Many cake recipes work well using this method, but others may not be so successful. Pastry does not work well. Breads work very well, perhaps because the amount of fat is usually relatively small, as do some cookies and bars, such as brownies and flapjacks.

To make the dried fruit purée to use in recipes, chop 4 ounces ready-to-eat dried fruit and place in a blender or food processor with 5 tablespoons water and blend to a roughly smooth purée. Then, simply substitute the same weight of this dried fruit purée for all or just some of the amount of fat in the recipe. The purée will keep in the fridge for up to three days.

You can use prunes, dried apricots, dried peaches, or dried apples, or substitute mashed fresh fruit, such as ripe bananas or lightly cooked apples, without the added water.

Above: A selection of cooking oils and low fat spreads. Always check the packaging of low fat spreads – for cooking, they must have a fat content of about 40%.

LOW FAT AND VERY LOW FAT SNACKS

Instead of reaching for some chips, a high fat cookie or a chocolate bar when hunger strikes, choose one of these tasty low fat snacks to fill that hungry hole.

● A piece of fresh fruit or vegetable such as an apple, banana or carrot – keep chunks or sticks wrapped in a plastic bag in the fridge.

● Fresh fruit or vegetable chunks – skewer them on to toothpicks or short bamboo skewers to make them into mini kebabs.

● A handful of dried fruit such as raisins, apricots or sultanas. These also make a perfect addition to children's lunch boxes or to school break snacks.

● A portion of canned fruit in natural fruit juice – serve with a spoonful or two of fat-free yogurt.

● One or two crisp rice cakes – delicious on their own, or topped with honey, or reduced fat cheese.

● Crackers, such as water biscuits or crisp breads, spread with reduced sugar jam or marmalade.

● A bowl of whole-wheat breakfast cereal or no-added-sugar granola served with a little skimmed milk.

● Very low fat plain or fruit yogurt or ricotta cheese.

● A toasted teacake spread with reduced sugar jam or marmalade.

● Toasted pancake spread with fruit purée.

MINIMIZING OIL IN COOKING

For fat-free or low fat cooking, it's best to avoid roasting and frying, both of which soak oil into the food. Choose instead to poach, grill, bake, steam or microwave, all of which are successful ways of cooking without adding fat.

Below are some more handy techniques that may be used for reducing or eliminating the amount of oil used in cooking. If you do need a little fat for cooking, choose an oil that is high in unsaturates, such as olive or sunflower oil.

TECHNIQUE	GOOD FOR	HOW TO
SWEATING VEGETABLES	Panfrying any vegetables, such as onions, mushrooms, carrots and celery, which would often be initially fried in oil or butter, as the basis of many savory recipes.	Put the sliced vegetables into a nonstick saucepan or frying pan with about ²/₃ cup low fat stock. Cover and cook for 5 minutes or until the vegetables are tender and the stock has reduced. If you like, add 1 tablespoon dry wine or wine vinegar for a little piquancy and continue cooking for a few minutes more until the vegetables are dry and lightly browned.
MARINATING	Adding flavor as well as helping to tenderize and keep food moist during cooking without adding any fat. Useful for meat, fish, poultry and vegetables. The marinade may also be used to baste the food while cooking or added to an accompanying sauce.	Soy sauce, vinegar, citrus juices and yogurt all make excellent fat-free marinade bases with herbs and spices added for extra flavor. Leave for at least 30 minutes, preferably overnight.
PARCEL COOKING	Fish, chicken, vegetables and fruit, allowing the food to cook in its own juices and the steam created, holding in all the flavor and nutrient value and eliminating the need for oil or fats.	Enclose food in individual foil or waxed paper or parchment packages, add extra flavorings such as wine, herbs and spices, if desired, twist or fold the package ends to secure and ensure that juices can't run out, then either bake, steam or cook on a grill.
SEARING	Sealing the juices into meat and poultry. Even lean cuts trimmed of skin and visible fat contain some hidden fat, so adding extra fat isn't necessary.	Place the meat in a heavy pan over moderate heat and cook on all sides until evenly browned all over. If the meat is particularly lean and sticks slightly, remove from the pan, brush or spray a little oil onto the pan's surface, heat then return the meat to the pan. Any excess fat that comes out of the meat may be drained off before continuing with the recipe.

LOW FAT STOCKS

A good homemade stock is invaluable in the kitchen, forming the basis for many soups, appetizers and main course dishes. Below are two low fat stock recipes that are economical and easy to make.

You could add poultry giblets to the chicken stock and vary the ingredients in the vegetable stock according to taste and availability. Both can be frozen until required; the chicken up to 6 months, the vegetarian up to 1 month.

CHICKEN STOCK

INGREDIENTS

Makes about 6 cups
2¹/₄ pounds chicken wings or thighs, skinned
1 onion
2 whole cloves
1 bay leaf
1 sprig of thyme
3–4 sprigs of parsley
10 black peppercorns

1 Cut the skinned chicken into pieces, then put them into a large, heavy saucepan. Peel the onion and stick with the cloves. Tie the bay leaf, thyme, parsley and peppercorns in a piece of cheesecloth and add to the saucepan together with the onion.

2 Pour in 7¹/₂ cups of cold water and bring slowly to simmering point. Skim off any scum with a slotted spoon, then continue to simmer very gently, uncovered, for 1¹/₂ hours. Strain the stock through a sieve into a large bowl and let sit until cool.

3 When cold, remove with a spoon the layer of fat that will have set on the surface.

> **COOK'S TIP**
>
> To make fish stock, follow the recipe for chicken stock, substituting fish bones, heads or trimmings for the chicken, and let simmer for 20–30 minutes.

VEGETABLE STOCK

INGREDIENTS

Makes about 6 cups
2 carrots
2 celery sticks
2 onions
2 tomatoes
10 mushroom stalks
2 bay leaves
1 sprig of thyme
3–4 sprigs of parsley
10 black peppercorns

1 Chop the carrots, celery, onions, tomatoes and mushroom stalks. Place them in a large heavy saucepan. Tie the remaining ingredients in a piece of cheesecloth and add to the pan.

2 Pour in 7¹/₂ cups cold water. Slowly bring to simmering point. Continue to simmer very gently, uncovered, for 1¹/₂ hours.

3 Strain through a sieve into a large bowl and let sit until cool. Keep in the refrigerator until required, or freeze in usable amounts.

LOW FAT SAUCES

Sauces can introduce an unwelcome amount of fat into a recipe, so that dishes that start out low in fat may end up being served in a rich, high fat coating. Unfortunately, it is not possible to simply introduce a low fat spread into most sauce recipes. The traditional roux method for making a sauce won't work successfully using low fat spreads because of their high water content, which will evaporate on heating, leaving insufficient fat to blend with the flour. Below, however, are three quick and easy low fat cooking methods to use, plus some alternatives to classic sauces.

● The All-in-One Method:
Place 2 tablespoons each of low fat spread and plain flour in a saucepan with 1¹/₄ cups skim milk. Bring to a boil, stirring constantly until the sauce is thickened and smooth.

● Using Stock to Replace Fat:
Sweat vegetables, such as onions and mushrooms, in a small amount of stock rather than frying in fat.

● Using Cornstarch to Thicken:
Blend 1 tablespoon cornstarch with 1–2 tablespoons cold water, then whisk into 1¹/₄ cup simmering stock or milk, bring to a boil and cook for 1 minute, stirring constantly.

LOW FAT VARIATIONS OF CLASSIC SAUCES

● Mayonnaise – You can buy commercially made reduced-calorie mayonnaise or to make further fat and calorie savings, substitute half the stated quantity with low fat plain yogurt or low fat fromage frais. This works well for mayonnaise-based dips or dressings such as Thousand Island, which have tomato paste or ketchup added.

● Hollandaise – This sauce is classically made with egg yolks, butter and vinegar and can't be made with low fat spreads. However, some fat saving can be made by using less butter and including buttermilk. Place 3 egg yolks in a bowl with the grated rind and 1 tablespoon juice from 1 lemon. Heat gently over a pan of water, stirring until thickened. Gradually whisk in 6 tablespoons softened butter, in small pieces, until smooth. Whisk in 3 tablespoons buttermilk and season. Reserve for special occasions.

Alternatively, flavor plain yogurt with a little French mustard and a little vinaigrette dressing and use to drizzle over asparagus.

● Vinaigrette Dressings – Buy reduced-calorie and oil-free dressings or, if you like the real thing, simply use less.

● Oil-Free Dressings – Whisk together 6 tablespoons low fat natural yogurt and 2 tablespoons freshly squeezed lemon juice, and season to taste with freshly ground black pepper. If you prefer, wine, cider or even orange juice could be used in place of the lemon juice. Add chopped fresh herbs, crushed garlic, mustard, honey, grated horseradish or other flavorings, if you like.

● Using Vegetable Purées for Thickening – Many recipes for sauces are traditionally thickened by adding cream, beurre manié (a butter and flour paste) or egg yolks, all of which add unwanted fat to the sauce. If cooked vegetables are included in the recipe, blend some down in a food processor to make a purée then stir back into the juices to produce a thickened sauce. Good for casserole sauces.

LOW FAT DESSERT OPTIONS

Desserts needn't be banned from a low fat diet. Many traditional dairy products are high in fat but it's a simple matter to adapt recipes and use low fat alternatives to create delicious results. Below are some simple low fat alternatives to using real dairy whipped cream that can be served with puddings or used for decorating cakes and desserts. Strained yogurt is lower in fat than many commercial varieties and is delicious served with puddings.

LOW FAT WHIPPED CREAM

— INGREDIENTS —

Makes ²/₃ cup
¹/₂ teaspoon powdered gelatin
5 tablespoons cold water
¹/₄ cup skim milk powder
1 tablespoon superfine sugar
1 tablespoon lemon juice

1 Sprinkle the powdered gelatin over 1 tablespoon of the water in a small bowl and let sit to "sponge" for 5 minutes. Place the bowl over a saucepan of hot water and stir until dissolved. Let cool.

2 Whisk the milk powder, sugar, lemon juice and remaining water until frothy. Add the dissolved gelatin and whisk. Chill for 30 minutes.

3 Whisk the chilled mixture again until very thick and frothy. Serve within 30 minutes of making.

YOGURT PIPING CREAM

— INGREDIENTS —

Makes scant 2 cups
2 teaspoons powdered gelatin
1¹/₄ cups strained yogurt
1 tablespoon sugar
¹/₂ teaspoon vanilla extract
1 egg white

1 Sprinkle the powdered gelatin over 3 tablespoons cold water in a small bowl and leave to "sponge" for 5 minutes. Place the bowl over a saucepan of hot water and stir until dissolved. Let cool.

2 Mix together the yogurt, sugar and vanilla extract. Stir in the gelatin. Chill for 30 minutes, or until just beginning to set around the edges.

3 Whisk the egg white until stiff and carefully fold it into the yogurt mixture. Spoon into a piping bag and use immediately.

STRAINED YOGURT AND SIMPLE CURD CHEESE

● To make strained yogurt: line a nylon or stainless–steel sieve with a double layer of cheesecloth. Set over a bowl and pour in 2¹/₂ cups low fat yogurt. Leave to drain in the refrigerator for 3 hours – it will have separated into thick, strained yogurt and watery whey. If desired, sweeten the yogurt with a little honey.
● To make curd cheese: allow the yogurt to drain for 8 hours or overnight. Spoon the curd cheese into a bowl, cover and chill until required. Use instead of sour cream, cream cheese or butter. Makes ¹/₂ cup.

THE FAT AND CALORIE CONTENTS OF FOOD

The following figures show the weight of fat (g) and the energy content per 100g/3.5oz of each food.

VEGETABLES

	FAT (g)	ENERGY		FAT (g)	ENERGY
Broccoli	0.9	33 Kcals/138 kJ	Peas	1.5	83 Kcals/344 kJ
Cabbage	0.4	26 Kcals/109 kJ	Potatoes	0.2	75 Kcals/318 kJ
Carrots	0.3	35 Kcals/146 kJ	Fries, home-made	6.7	189 Kcals/796 kJ
Cauliflower	0.9	34 Kcals/142 kJ	Fries, retail	12.4	239 Kcals/1001 kJ
Cucumber	0.1	10 Kcals/40 kJ	Oven-chips, frozen, baked	4.2	162 Kcals/687 kJ
Mushrooms	0.5	13 Kcals/55 kJ	Tomatoes	0.3	17 Kcals/73 kJ
Onions	0.2	36 Kcals/151 kJ	Zucchini	0.4	18 Kcals/74 kJ

BEANS AND LEGUMES

	FAT (g)	ENERGY		FAT (g)	ENERGY
Black-eyed peas, cooked	1.8	116 Kcals/494 kJ	Lima beans, canned	0.5	77 Kcals/327 kJ
Chick-peas, canned	2.9	115 Kcals/487 kJ	Red kidney beans, canned	0.6	100 Kcals/424 kJ
Hummus	12.6	187 Kcals/781 kJ	Red lentils, cooked	0.4	100 Kcals/424 kJ

FISH AND SEAFOOD

	FAT (g)	ENERGY		FAT (g)	ENERGY
Cod fillets, fresh	0.7	80 Kcals/337 kJ	Shrimp	0.9	99 Kcals/418 kJ
Crab, canned	0.5	77 Kcals/326 kJ	Trout, grilled	5.4	135 Kcals/565 kJ
Haddock, fresh	0.6	81 Kcals/345 kJ	Tuna, canned in water	0.6	99 Kcals/422 kJ
Lemon sole, fresh	1.5	83 Kcals/351 kJ	Tuna, canned in oil	9.0	189 Kcals/794 kJ

MEAT PRODUCTS

	FAT (g)	ENERGY		FAT (g)	ENERGY
Bacon strip	39.5	414 Kcals/1710 kJ	Chicken fillet, raw	1.1	106 Kcals/449 kJ
Turkey bacon strip	1.0	99 Kcals/414 kJ	Chicken, roasted	12.5	218 Kcals/910 kJ
Beef, ground, raw	16.2	225 Kcals/934 kJ	Duck, meat only, raw	6.5	137 Kcals/575 kJ
Beef, ground, extra lean, raw	9.6	174 Kcals/728 kJ	Duck, roasted, meat, fat and skin	38.1	423 Kcals/1750 kJ
Rump steak, lean and marbled	10.1	174 Kcals/726 kJ	Turkey, meat only, raw	1.6	105 Kcals/443 kJ
Rump steak, lean only	4.1	125 Kcals/526 kJ	Liver, lamb, raw	6.2	137 Kcals/575 kJ
Lamb chops, loin, lean and fat	23.0	277 Kcals/1150 kJ	Pork pie	27.0	376 Kcals/1564 kJ
Lamb, average, lean, raw	8.3	156 Kcals/651 kJ	Salami	45.2	491 Kcals/2031 kJ
Pork chops, loin, lean and fat	21.7	270 Kcals/1119 kJ	Sausage roll, flaky pastry	36.4	477 Kcals/1985 kJ
Pork, average, lean, raw	4.0	123 Kcals/519 kJ			

DAIRY, FATS AND OILS

	FAT (g)	ENERGY		FAT (g)	ENERGY
Cream, heavy	48.0	449 Kcals/1849 kJ	Greek yogurt	9.1	115 Kcals/477 kJ
Cream, light	19.1	198 Kcals/817 kJ	Reduced fat Greek yogurt	5.0	80 Kcals/335 kJ
Cream, whipping	39.3	373 Kcals/1539 kJ	Butter	81.7	737 Kcals/3031 kJ
Crème fraîche	40.0	379 Kcals/1567 kJ	Margarine	81.6	739 Kcals/3039 kJ
Reduced fat crème fraîche	15.0	165 Kcals/683 kJ	Low fat spread	40.5	390 Kcals/1605 kJ
Reduced fat heavy cream	24.0	243 Kcals/1002 kJ	Very low fat spread	25	273 Kcals/1128 kJ
Milk, skim	0.1	33 Kcals/130 kJ	Shortening	99.0	891 Kcals/3663 kJ
Milk, whole	3.9	66 Kcals/275 kJ	Corn oil	99.9	899 Kcals/3696 kJ
Brie	26.9	319 Kcals/1323 kJ	Olive oil	99.9	899 Kcals/3696 kJ
Cheddar cheese	34.4	412 Kcals/1708 kJ	Safflower oil	99.9	899 Kcals/3696 kJ
Cheddar-type, reduced fat	15.0	261 Kcals/1091 kJ	Eggs	10.8	147 Kcals/612 kJ
Cream cheese	47.4	439 Kcals/1807 kJ	Egg yolk	30.5	339 Kcals/1402 kJ
Skimmed milk soft cheese	7.1	113 Kcals/469 kJ	Egg white	Trace	36 Kcals/153 kJ
Edam cheese	25.4	333 Kcals/1382 kJ	Fat-free dressing	1.2	67 Kcals/282 kJ
Feta cheese	20.2	250 Kcals/1037 kJ	French dressing	49.4	462 Kcals/1902 kJ
Parmesan cheese	32.7	452 Kcals/1880 kJ	Mayonnaise	75.6	691 Kcals/2843 kJ
Low fat yogurt, plain	0.8	56 Kcals/236 kJ	Mayonnaise, reduced calorie	28.1	288 Kcals/1188 kJ

CEREALS, BAKING AND PRESERVES

	FAT (g)	ENERGY		FAT (g)	ENERGY
Brown rice, uncooked	2.8	357 Kcals/1518 kJ	Flapjack	26.6	484 Kcals/2028 kJ
White rice, uncooked	3.6	383 K/cals/1630 kJ	Shortbread	26.1	498 Kcals/2087 kJ
Pasta, white, uncooked	1.8	342 Kcals/1456 kJ	Spongecake	16.9	393 Kcals/1652 kJ
Pasta, whole-wheat, uncooked	2.5	324 Kcal/1379 kJ	Fatless spongecake	6.1	294 Kcals/1245 kJ
Brown bread	2.0	218 Kcals/927 kJ	Doughnut, jelly	14.5	336 Kcals/1414 kJ
White bread	1.9	235 Kcals/1002 kJ	Sugar, white	0	105 Kcals/394 kJ
Whole-wheat bread	2.5	215 Kcals/914 kJ	Chocolate, sweet	30.3	520 Kcals/2214 kJ
Cornflakes	0.7	360 Kcals/1535 kJ	Chocolate, semisweet	29.2	510 Kcals/2157 kJ
Raisin bran	1.6	303 Kcals/1289 kJ	Honey	0	288 Kcals/1229 kJ
Swiss-style granola	5.9	363 Kcals/1540 kJ	Lemon curd	5.1	283 Kcals/1202 kJ
Croissant	20.3	360 Kcals/1505 kJ	Fruit jam	0	261 Kcals/1116 kJ

FRUIT AND NUTS

	FAT (g)	ENERGY		FAT (g)	ENERGY
Apples	0.1	47 Kcals/199 kJ	Pears	0.1	40 Kcals/169 kJ
Avocados	19.5	190 Kcals/784 kJ	Almonds	55.8	612 Kcals/2534 kJ
Bananas	0.3	95 Kcals/403 kJ	Brazil nuts	68.2	682 Kcals/2813 kJ
Dried mixed fruit	0.4	268 Kcals/1114 kJ	Hazelnuts	63.5	650 Kcals/2685 kJ
Grapefruit	0.1	30 Kcals/126 kJ	Pine nuts	68.6	688 Kcals/2840 kJ
Oranges	0.1	37 Kcals/158 kJ	Walnuts	68.5	688 Kcals/2837 kJ
Peaches	0.1	33 Kcals/142 kJ	Peanut butter, smooth	53.7	623 Kcals/2581 kJ

SOUPS AND APPETIZERS

The wide variety of fresh ingredients available today makes it easy to create tempting soups and appetizers that are filling, nutritious and low in fat. The recipes in this section are versatile and easy to prepare, as well as being delicious. Hearty homemade soups, such as Corn Chowder with Pasta Shells or Vegetable Minestrone, served with a chunk of fresh crusty bread, are perfect as an appetizer, snack or light meal. Take advantage of the huge variety of fresh fruits and herbs now available to create fragrant, colorful, virtually fat-free starters such as Melon, Pineapple and Grape Cocktail and Mussels with Thai Herbs.

SPLIT PEA AND ZUCCHINI SOUP

Rich and satisfying, this tasty and nutritious soup will warm a chilly winter's day.

INGREDIENTS

Serves 4

1⅞ cups yellow split peas
1 medium onion, finely chopped
1 tsp sunflower oil
2 medium zucchini, finely diced
3¾ cups chicken broth
½ tsp ground turmeric
salt and black pepper

1 Place the split peas in a bowl, cover with cold water, and leave to soak for several hours or overnight. Drain, rinse in cold water, and drain again.

2 Cook the onion in the oil in a covered pan, shaking occasionally, until soft. Reserve a handful of diced zucchini and add the rest to the pan. Cook, stirring, for 2–3 minutes.

3 Add the broth and turmeric to the pan and bring to a boil. Reduce the heat, then cover and simmer for 30–40 minutes, or until the split peas are tender. Adjust the seasoning.

4 When the soup is almost ready, bring a large saucepan of water to a boil, add the reserved diced zucchini, and cook for 1 minute, then drain and add to the soup before serving hot with warm crusty bread.

COOK'S TIP
For a quicker alternative, use split red lentils for this soup – they need no pre-soaking and cook very quickly. Adjust the amount of broth, if necessary.

NUTRITION NOTES

Per portion:

Energy	174Kcals/730kJ
Fat	2.14g
Saturated fat	0.54g
Cholesterol	0
Fiber	3.43g

CHILLED FRESH TOMATO SOUP

This effortless uncooked soup can be made in minutes.

INGREDIENTS

Serves 6

3–3½ lb ripe tomatoes, peeled and
  coarsely chopped
4 garlic cloves, crushed
2 tbsp balsamic vinegar
4 thick slices whole-wheat bread
black pepper
low fat ricotta cheese, to garnish

1 Place the tomatoes in a blender with the garlic. Blend until smooth.

2 Press the mixture through a sieve to remove the seeds. Stir in the balsamic vinegar and season to taste with pepper. Put in the fridge to chill.

3 Toast the bread lightly on both sides. While still hot, cut off the crusts and slice the toast in half horizontally. Place on a board with the uncooked sides facing down and, using a circular motion, rub to remove any doughy pieces of bread.

COOK'S TIP
For the best flavor, it is important to use only fully-ripened, flavorful tomatoes in this soup.

4 Cut each slice into four triangles. Place on a broiler pan and toast the uncooked sides until lightly golden. Garnish each bowl of soup with a spoonful of ricotta cheese and serve with the Melba toast.

NUTRITION NOTES

Per portion:

Energy	111Kcals/475kJ
Fat	1.42g
Saturated fat	0.39g
Cholesterol	0.16mg
Fiber	4.16g

CORN CHOWDER WITH PASTA SHELLS

Smoked turkey bacon provides a tasty, low fat alternative to bacon in this hearty dish. If you prefer, omit the meat altogether and serve the soup as is.

INGREDIENTS

Serves 4

1 small green bell pepper
1 lb potatoes, peeled and diced
2 cups canned or frozen corn
1 onion, chopped
1 celery stalk, chopped
a bouquet garni (bay leaf, parsley stalks
   and thyme)
2½ cups chicken stock
1¼ cups skim milk
2oz small pasta shells
oil, for frying
5oz smoked turkey bacon strips, diced
salt and black pepper
breadsticks, to serve

NUTRITION NOTES	
Per portion:	
Energy	215Kcals/904kJ
Fat	1.6g
Saturated fat	0.3g
Cholesterol	13mg
Fiber	2.8g

1 Halve the green pepper, then remove the stalk and seeds. Cut the flesh into small dice, cover with boiling water and let stand for 2 minutes. Drain and rinse.

2 Put the potatoes into a saucepan with the corn, onion, celery, green pepper, bouquet garni and stock. Bring to a boil, cover and simmer for 20 minutes, until tender.

3 Add the milk and season with salt and pepper. Process half the soup in a food processor or blender and return to the pan with the pasta shells. Simmer for 10 minutes.

4 Fry the turkey bacon in a nonstick frying pan for 2–3 minutes. Stir into the soup. Season to taste and serve with breadsticks.

VEGETABLE MINESTRONE

INGREDIENTS

Serves 6–8
large pinch of saffron strands
1 onion, chopped
1 leek, sliced
1 stalk celery, sliced
2 carrots, diced
2–3 garlic cloves, crushed
2½ cups chicken stock
28oz can chopped tomatoes
½ cup frozen peas
2oz soup pasta (anellini)
1 tsp sugar
1 tbsp chopped fresh parsley
1 tbsp chopped fresh basil
salt and black pepper

1 Soak the pinch of saffron strands in 1 tablespoon boiling water. Allow to stand for 10 minutes.

2 Meanwhile, put the prepared onion, leek, celery, carrots and garlic into a large pan. Add the chicken stock, bring to a boil, cover and simmer for about 10 minutes.

3 Add the canned tomatoes, the saffron with its liquid and the frozen peas. Bring back to a boil and add the soup pasta. Simmer for 10 minutes until tender.

COOK'S TIP
Saffron strands aren't essential for this soup, but they give a wonderfully delicate flavor, with the bonus of a lovely rich orange-yellow color.

4 Season with sugar, salt and pepper to taste. Stir in the chopped herbs just before serving.

NUTRITION NOTES

Per portion:	
Energy	87Kcals/367kJ
Fat	0.7g
Saturated fat	0.1g
Cholesterol	0
Fiber	3.3g

SALMON PARCELS

Serve these little savory parcels just as they are for a snack, or with a pool of fresh tomato sauce for a special appetizer.

INGREDIENTS

Makes 12
3½oz can red or pink salmon
1 tbsp chopped fresh cilantro
4 scallions, finely chopped
4 sheets fila pastry
sunflower oil, for brushing
scallions and lettuce, to serve

COOK'S TIP
When you are using fila pastry, it is important to prevent it drying out; cover any you are not using with a dish towel or plastic wrap.

1 Preheat the oven to 400°F. Lightly oil a baking sheet. Drain the salmon, discarding any skin and bones, then place in a bowl.

2 Flake the salmon with a fork and mix with the fresh cilantro and scallions.

3 Place a single sheet of fila pastry on a work surface and brush lightly with oil. Place another sheet on top. Cut into six squares, each about 4in. Repeat with the remaining pastry, to make 12 squares.

4 Place a spoonful of the salmon mixture on each square. Brush the edges of the pastry with oil, then draw together, pressing to seal. Place on a baking sheet and bake for 12–15 minutes, until golden. Serve warm, with scallions and lettuce.

NUTRITION NOTES

Per portion:
Energy	25Kcals/107kJ
Fat	1.16g
Saturated fat	0.23g
Cholesterol	2.55mg
Fiber	0.05g

TOMATO-CHEESE TARTS

These crisp little tartlets are easier to make than they look. Best eaten fresh from the oven.

INGREDIENTS

Serves 4
2 sheets fila pastry
1 egg white
½ cup low fat cream cheese
handful fresh basil leaves
3 small tomatoes, sliced
salt and black pepper

1 Preheat the oven to 400°F. Brush the sheets of fila pastry lightly with egg white and cut into sixteen 4 in squares.

2 Layer the squares in twos, in eight muffin tins. Spoon the cheese into the pastry cases. Season with black pepper and top with basil leaves.

3 Arrange tomatoes on the tarts, add seasoning, and bake for 10-12 minutes, until golden. Serve warm.

NUTRITION NOTES

Per portion:
Energy	50Kcals/210kJ
Fat	0.33g
Saturated fat	0.05g
Cholesterol	0.29mg
Fiber	0.25g

MELON, PINEAPPLE AND GRAPE COCKTAIL

A light, refreshing fruit salad, with no added sugar and virtually no fat, perfect for breakfast or brunch – or any time.

INGREDIENTS

Serves 4

½ *melon*
8oz fresh or canned pineapple packed in juice
8oz seedless white grapes, halved
½ *cup white grape juice*
fresh mint leaves, to decorate (optional)

1 Remove the seeds from the melon half and use a melon baller to scoop out even-size balls.

2 Using a sharp knife, cut the skin from the pineapple and discard. Cut the fruit into bite-size chunks.

3 Combine all the fruits in a glass serving dish and add the grape juice. If you are using canned pineapple, measure the drained juice and bring it up to the required quantity with the grape juice.

4 If not serving immediately, cover and chill. Serve decorated with mint leaves, if desired.

NUTRITION NOTES

Per portion:

Energy	79Kcals/331kJ
Fat	0.2g
Saturated Fat	0
Cholesterol	0
Fiber	1.1g

CHILI TOMATO SALSA

This universal dip is great served with absolutely anything and can be made up to 24 hours in advance.

INGREDIENTS

Serves 4
1 shallot, peeled and halved
2 garlic cloves, peeled
handful of fresh basil leaves
1¼ lb ripe tomatoes
2 tsp olive oil
2 green chilies
salt and black pepper

1 Place the shallot and garlic in a food processor with the fresh basil. Blend the shallot, garlic and basil until finely chopped.

2 Halve the tomatoes and add to the food processor. Pulse the machine until the mixture is well blended and coarsely chopped.

3 With the motor running, slowly pour in the olive oil. Add salt and pepper to taste.

NUTRITION NOTES

Per portion:
Energy	28Kcals/79kJ
Fat	0.47g
Saturated fat	0.13g
Cholesterol	0
Fiber	1.45g

4 Halve the chilies lengthwise and remove the seeds. Finely slice the chilies across the width into tiny strips and stir into the tomato salsa. Serve at room temperature.

COOK'S TIP
The salsa is best made in the summer when tomatoes are at their best. In winter, use a drained 14oz can of plum tomatoes.

MUSSELS WITH THAI HERBS

Another simple dish to prepare. The lemongrass adds a refreshing tang to the mussels.

INGREDIENTS

Serves 6
2¼ lb mussels, cleaned and beards
    removed
2 lemongrass stalks, finely chopped
4 shallots, chopped
4 kafir lime leaves, coarsely torn
2 red chilies, sliced
1 tbsp fish sauce
2 tbsp lime juice
2 scallions, chopped, and
    cilantro leaves, to garnish

1 Put all the ingredients, except the scallions and cilantro, in a large saucepan and stir thoroughly.

2 Cover and cook for 5–7 minutes, shaking the saucepan occasionally, until the mussels open. Discard any mussels that do not open.

3 Transfer the cooked mussels to a serving platter.

4 Garnish the mussels with chopped scallions and cilantro leaves. Serve immediately.

NUTRITION NOTES	
Per portion:	
Energy	56Kcals/238kJ
Fat	1.22g
Saturated Fat	0.16g
Cholesterol	0.32mg
Fiber	0.27g

TOMATO-PESTO TOASTIES

Ready-made pesto is high in fat but, as its flavor is so powerful, it can be used in very small amounts with good effect, as in these tasty toasties.

INGREDIENTS

Serves 2
2 thick slices crusty bread
3 tbsp low fat cream cheese or low fat
   fromage frais
2 tsp red or green pesto
1 beefsteak tomato
1 red onion
salt and black pepper

1 Place the bread slices under a hot broiler until golden brown on both sides, turning once. Leave to cool.

2 Mix together the low fat cream cheese and pesto in a small bowl until well blended, then spread thickly on the toasted bread.

3 Cut the beefsteak tomato and red onion, crosswise, into thin slices using a large sharp knife.

4 Arrange the slices, overlapping, on top of the toast and season with salt and pepper. Transfer the toasties to a broiler pan and broil until heated through, then serve immediately.

COOK'S TIP
Almost any type of crusty bread can be used for this recipe, but Italian olive oil bread and French bread will give the best flavor.

NUTRITION NOTES
Per portion:

Energy	177Kcals/741kJ
Fat	2.41g
Saturated fat	0.19g
Cholesterol	0.23mg
Fiber	2.2g

PASTA, BEANS AND GRAINS

Pasta, beans and grains on their own are low in fat and a good source of carbohydrate, but they are often prepared with high fat ingredients and sauces. It is possible, however, to prepare appetizing low fat meals by creatively combining pasta, beans and grains with flavorful ingredients and cooking them according to low fat guidelines. There are old favorites to choose from, including pasta classics such as Spaghetti alla Carbonara and Tagliatelle with Mushrooms, and new, exciting combinations, such as Minted Couscous Castles and Spicy Bean Hot Pot.

SPAGHETTI WITH CHILI BEAN SAUCE

A nutritious vegetarian option, ideal as a low-fat main course.

INGREDIENTS

Serves 6

1 onion, finely chopped
1–2 garlic cloves, crushed
1 large green chili, seeded
  and chopped
2/3 cup vegetable stock
1 14oz can chopped tomatoes
2 tbsp tomato paste
1/2 cup red wine
1 tsp dried oregano
7 ounces green beans, sliced
1 14oz can red kidney
  beans, drained
1 14oz can cannellini
  beans, drained
1 14oz can chickpeas, drained
1 lb spaghetti
salt and black pepper

NUTRITION NOTES	
Per portion:	
Energy	431Kcals/1811kJ
Fat	3.6g
Saturated fat	0.2g
Cholesterol	0
Fiber	9.9g

1 To make the sauce, put the chopped onion, garlic and chili into a non-stick pan with the stock. Bring to a boil and cook for 5 minutes, until tender.

2 Add the tomatoes, tomato paste, wine, seasoning and oregano. Bring to a boil, cover and simmer the sauce for 20 minutes.

3 Cook the green beans in boiling, salted water for about 5–6 minutes, until tender. Drain thoroughly.

4 Add all the beans and the chickpeas to the sauce and simmer for another 10 minutes. Meanwhile, cook the spaghetti in a large pot of boiling, salted water according to the individual package instructions, until *al dente*. Drain thoroughly. Transfer the pasta to a serving dish or plates and top with the chili bean sauce.

> **COOK'S TIP**
> Rinse canned beans thoroughly under cold, running water to remove as much salt as possible, and drain well before use.

SPAGHETTI ALLA CARBONARA

This is a variation on the classic charcoal-burner's spaghetti, using turkey bacon and low fat cream cheese instead of the traditional bacon and egg.

INGREDIENTS

Serves 4
5oz smoked turkey bacon
oil, for frying
1 medium onion, chopped
1–2 garlic cloves, crushed
⅔ cup chicken stock
⅔ cup dry white wine
7oz low fat cream cheese
1 lb chili and garlic-flavored spaghetti
2 tbsp chopped fresh parsley
salt and black pepper
shavings of Parmesan cheese,
  to serve

1 Cut the turkey bacon into ½in strips. Fry quickly in a nonstick pan for 2–3 minutes. Add the onion, garlic and stock to the pan. Bring to a boil, cover and simmer for about 5 minutes, until tender.

COOK'S TIP
If you can't find chili and garlic-flavored spaghetti, use plain spaghetti and add a small amount of fresh chili and garlic in step 4 or use the pasta of your choice.

2 Add the wine and boil rapidly until reduced by half. Whisk in the cream cheese and season to taste.

3 Meanwhile, cook the spaghetti in a large pot of boiling, salted water for 10–12 minutes, until *al dente*. Drain thoroughly.

4 Return the spaghetti to the pan with the sauce and parsley, toss well and serve immediately with a few thin shavings of Parmesan cheese.

NUTRITION NOTES	
Per portion:	
Energy	500Kcals/2102kJ
Fat	3.3g
Saturated fat	0.5g
Cholesterol	21mg
Fiber	4g

Tagliatelle with Mushrooms

INGREDIENTS

Serves 4

1 small onion, finely chopped
2 garlic cloves, crushed
⅔ cup vegetable stock
8oz mixed fresh mushrooms, such as
  portobello, oyster or chanterelles
4 tbsp white or red wine
2 tsp tomato paste
1 tbsp soy sauce
1 tsp chopped fresh thyme
2 tbsp chopped fresh parsley, plus extra
  to garnish
8oz fresh sun-dried tomato and herb
  tagliatelle
salt and black pepper
shavings of Parmesan cheese, to serve
  (optional)

1 Put the onion and garlic into a pan with the stock, then cover and cook for 5 minutes or until tender.

NUTRITION NOTES	
Per portion:	
Energy	226Kcals/961kJ
Fat	1.5g
Saturated Fat	0.7g
Cholesterol	0
Fiber	2.9g

2 Add the mushrooms (quartered or sliced if large or left whole if small), wine, tomato paste and soy sauce. Cover and cook for 5 minutes.

3 Remove the lid from the pan and boil until the liquid has reduced by half. Stir in the chopped fresh herbs and season to taste.

4 Cook the fresh pasta in a large pot of boiling, salted water for 2–5 minutes, until *al dente*. Drain thoroughly and toss lightly with the mushrooms. Serve, garnished with parsley and shavings of Parmesan cheese, if desired.

BAKED RATATOUILLE WITH PENNE

INGREDIENTS

Serves 6

1 small eggplant
2 zucchini, thickly sliced
7oz firm tofu, cubed
3 tablespoons dark soy sauce
1 garlic clove, crushed
2 tsp sesame seeds
1 red bell pepper, seeded and sliced
1 onion, finely chopped
1–2 garlic cloves, crushed
²⁄₃ cup vegetable stock
3 firm ripe tomatoes, skinned, seeded
    and quartered
1 tbsp chopped mixed herbs
8oz penne or other pasta shapes
salt and black pepper
crusty bread, to serve

1 Wash the eggplant and cut into 1in cubes. Put into a colander with the zucchini, sprinkle with salt and allow to drain for 30 minutes.

2 Mix the tofu with the soy sauce, garlic and sesame seeds. Cover and marinate for 30 minutes.

3 Put the pepper, onion and garlic into a saucepan with the stock. Bring to a boil, cover and cook for 5 minutes until tender. Remove the lid and boil until all the stock has evaporated. Add the tomatoes and herbs to the pan and cook for another 3 minutes, then add the rinsed eggplant and zucchini and cook until tender. Season to taste.

COOK'S TIP
Tofu is a low-fat protein, but it is very bland. Marinating adds plenty of flavor – make sure you leave it for the full 30 minutes.

4 Meanwhile, cook the pasta in a large pot of boiling, salted water according to the package instructions, until *al dente*, then drain thoroughly. Preheat the broiler. Toss the pasta with the vegetables and tofu. Transfer to a shallow ovenproof dish and broil until lightly toasted. Serve with bread.

NUTRITION NOTES
Per portion:

Energy	208Kcals/873kJ
Fat	3.7g
Saturated fat	0.5g
Cholesterol	0
Fiber	3.9g

BEAN PASTE WITH BROILED ENDIVE

The slightly bitter flavors of the radicchio and endive make a wonderful marriage with the creamy bean paste. Walnut oil adds a nutty taste, but olive oil could also be used.

INGREDIENTS

Serves 4
1 14oz can cannellini beans
3 tbsp low fat ricotta cheese
finely grated rind and juice of
*   1 large orange*
1 tbsp finely chopped
*   fresh rosemary*
4 Belgian endives
2 medium heads radicchio
2 tbsp walnut oil
shreds of orange rind, to garnish
*   (optional)*

COOK'S TIP
Other suitable beans to use are navy, mung or broad beans.

1 Drain the beans, rinse, and drain again. Pulse the beans in a blender or food processor with the ricotta cheese, orange rind, orange juice and rosemary. Set aside.

2 Cut the heads of endive in half lengthwise.

3 Cut each radicchio head into eight wedges. Preheat the broiler.

4 Lay out the endive and radicchio on a baking tray and brush with the walnut oil. Broil for 2–3 minutes. Serve with the bean paste and sprinkle with the orange shreds, if using.

NUTRITION NOTES	
Per portion:	
Energy	110Kcals/464kJ
Fat	2.5g
Saturated Fat	0.15g
Cholesterol	0.1mg
Fiber	5.3g

SPICY BEAN HOT POT

INGREDIENTS

Serves 4

3 cups button mushrooms
1 tbsp sunflower oil
2 onions, sliced
1 garlic clove, crushed
1 tbsp red wine vinegar
1 14oz can chopped tomatoes
1 tbsp tomato paste
1 tbsp Worcestershire sauce
1 tbsp whole-grain mustard
1 tbsp dark brown sugar
1 cup vegetable stock
1 14oz can red kidney beans,
  drained
1 14oz can cannellini beans,
  drained
1 bay leaf
½ cup raisins
salt and black pepper
chopped fresh parsley, to garnish

1 Wipe the mushrooms, then cut them into small pieces. Set aside.

2 Heat the oil in a large saucepan or flameproof casserole, add the onions and garlic and cook over low heat for 10 minutes until soft.

3 Add all the remaining ingredients except the mushrooms and seasoning. Bring to a boil, lower the heat and simmer for 10 minutes.

4 Add the mushrooms and simmer for 5 more minutes. Stir in salt and pepper to taste. Transfer to warm plates and sprinkle with parsley.

NUTRITION NOTES	
Per portion:	
Energy	278Kcals/1169kJ
Fat	4.5g
Saturated Fat	0.55g
Cholesterol	0
Fiber	11.1g

VEGETABLE BIRYANI

This exotic dish made from everyday ingredients will be appreciated by vegetarians and meat-eaters alike. It is extremely low in fat, but packed full of exciting flavors.

INGREDIENTS

Serves 4–6
1 cup long-grain rice
2 whole cloves
seeds of 2 cardamom pods
2 cups vegetable stock
2 garlic cloves
1 small onion, coarsely chopped
1 tsp cumin seeds
1 tsp ground coriander
½ tsp ground turmeric
½ tsp chili powder
1 large potato, peeled and cut into
*   1in cubes*
2 carrots, sliced
½ cauliflower, broken into florets
2oz green beans, cut into
*   1in lengths*
2 tbsp chopped cilantro
2 tbsp lime juice
salt and black pepper
sprig of cilantro, to garnish

NUTRITION NOTES

Per portion:
Energy	175Kcals/737kJ
Fat	0.78g
Saturated Fat	0.12g
Cholesterol	0
Fiber	0.58g

COOK'S TIP
Substitute other vegetables, if you like. Zucchini, broccoli, parsnip and sweet potatoes would all be excellent choices.

4 Preheat the oven to 350°F. Spoon the spicy paste into a large flameproof casserole and cook over low heat for about 2 minutes, stirring occasionally.

5 Add the potato, carrots, cauliflower florets, beans and 6 tbsp water. Cover and cook over low heat for 12 more minutes, stirring occasionally. Add the chopped cilantro.

2 Reduce the heat, cover and simmer for 20 minutes, or until all the stock has been absorbed.

6 Remove the cloves and spoon the rice over the vegetables. Sprinkle with the lime juice. Cover and cook in the oven for 25 minutes, or until the vegetables are tender. Fluff up the rice with a fork before serving and garnish with a sprig of fresh cilantro.

1 Put the rice, cloves and cardamom seeds into a large, heavy saucepan. Pour in the stock and bring to a boil.

3 Meanwhile put the garlic cloves, onion, cumin seeds, coriander, ground turmeric, chili powder and seasoning into a blender or coffee grinder with 2 tablespoons water. Blend to a smooth paste.

COCONUT RICE

A delicious alternative to plain boiled rice. Brown or white rice will both work well.

―――――― INGREDIENTS ――――――

Serves 6
2 cups long-grain rice
1 cup water
2 cups coconut milk
½ tsp salt
2 tbsp sugar
fresh shredded coconut, to garnish

1 Wash the rice in cold water until it runs clear. Place water, coconut milk, salt and sugar in a heavy saucepan or flameproof casserole.

COOK'S TIP
Coconut milk is available in cans, but if you cannot find it, use creamed coconut mixed with water according to the package instructions.

2 Add the rice, cover and bring to a boil. Reduce the heat to low and simmer for 15–20 minutes or until the rice is tender to the bite and cooked through.

3 Turn off the heat and allow the rice to rest in the saucepan for another 5–10 minutes.

4 Fluff up the rice with chopsticks or a fork before serving garnished with shredded coconut.

―――――― NUTRITION NOTES ――――――

Per portion:
Energy	322.5Kcals/1371kJ
Fat	2.49g
Saturated fat	1.45g
Cholesterol	0
Fiber	0.68g

MINTED COUSCOUS CASTLES

Couscous is a fine semolina flour made from wheat grain, which is usually steamed and served plain with a rich meat or vegetable stew. Here it is flavored with mint and molded to make an unusual accompaniment to serve with any savory dish.

INGREDIENTS

Serves 6

1¼ cups couscous
2 cups boiling broth
1 tbsp lemon juice
2 tomatoes, diced
2 tbsp chopped fresh mint
oil, for brushing
salt and black pepper
mint sprigs, to garnish

1 Place the couscous in a bowl and pour over the boiling broth. Cover the bowl and leave to stand for 30 minutes, until all the broth is absorbed and the grains are tender.

2 Stir in the lemon juice with the tomatoes and chopped mint. Adjust the seasoning with salt and pepper.

3 Brush the insides of four cups or individual molds with oil. Spoon in the couscous mixture and pack down firmly. Chill for several hours.

4 Turn out and serve cold, or alternatively, cover and heat gently in a low oven or microwave, then turn out and serve hot, garnished with mint.

> COOK'S TIP
> Most couscous is now the ready-cooked variety, which can be cooked as above, but some types need steaming first, so check the package instructions.

NUTRITION NOTES

Per portion:
Energy	95Kcals/397kJ
Fat	0.53g
Saturated fat	0.07g
Cholesterol	0
Fiber	0.29g

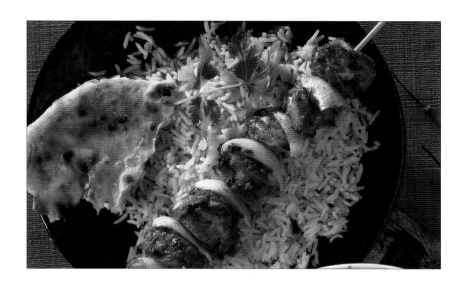

MEAT AND POULTRY

There is no reason why meat should not be a valuable part of a low fat diet. Make the most of the many leaner cuts of meat available today and utilize low fat preparation and cooking methods to make delicious, low fat dishes. Most poultry, especially chicken and turkey, is naturally low in fat, making it ideal for a low fat diet. Included here are a wide range of tasty and nutritious main courses, all packed with flavor. Try Turkey and Pasta Bake, perfect for feeding a family; spicy Tandoori Chicken Skewers for an al fresco summer lunch and Venison with Cranberry Sauce for a special occasion dinner.

CHICKEN, CARROT AND LEEK PACKAGES

These intriguing packages may sound a bit fussy for everyday eating, but actually they take very little time, and you can freeze them so they'll be ready to cook when needed.

INGREDIENTS

Serves 4

4 chicken fillets or skinless, boneless breasts
2 small leeks, sliced
2 carrots, grated
2 pitted black olives, chopped
1 garlic clove, crushed
4 anchovy fillets, halved lengthwise
salt and black pepper
black olives and herb sprigs, to garnish

1 Preheat the oven to 400°F. Season the chicken well.

2 Cut out four sheets of lightly greased parchment paper about 9in square. Divide the leeks equally among them. Put a piece of chicken on top of each.

3 Stir together the carrots, olives and garlic. Season lightly and place on top of the chicken portions. Top each with two of the anchovy fillets.

4 Carefully wrap up each package, making sure the paper folds are sealed. Bake for 20 minutes and serve hot, in the paper, garnished with black olives and herb sprigs.

NUTRITION NOTES

Per portion:

Energy	154Kcals/651kJ
Fat	2.37g
Saturated fat	0.45g
Cholesterol	78.75mg
Fiber	2.1g

COOK'S TIP
Skinless, boneless chicken is low in fat and is an excellent source of protein. Small, skinless turkey breast fillets also work well in this recipe and make a tasty change.

RAGOÛT OF VEAL

If you are looking for a low-calorie dish to treat yourself – or some guests – then this is perfect, and quick, too.

INGREDIENTS

Serves 4

12oz veal cutlets or loin
2 tsp olive oil
10–12 tiny onions, kept whole
1 yellow bell pepper, seeded and
  cut into eighths
1 orange or red bell pepper, seeded
  and cut into eighths
3 tomatoes, peeled
  and quartered
4 fresh basil sprigs
2 tbsp dry vermouth or sherry
salt and black pepper

NUTRITION NOTES

Per portion:
Energy	158Kcals/665.5kJ
Fat	4.97g
Saturated Fat	1.14g
Cholesterol	63mg
Fiber	2.5g

1 Trim off any fat and cut the veal into cubes. Heat the oil in a frying pan and gently stir-fry the veal and onions until browned.

2 After a couple of minutes, add the peppers and tomatoes. Continue stir-frying for another 4–5 minutes.

COOK'S TIP
Lean beef or pork fillet may be used instead of veal, if you prefer. Shallots can replace the onions.

3 Add half the basil leaves, coarsely chopped (keep some for garnish), the vermouth or sherry, and seasoning. Cook, stirring frequently, for another 10 minutes, or until the meat is tender.

4 Sprinkle with the remaining basil leaves and serve hot.

VENISON WITH CRANBERRY SAUCE

Venison steaks are now widely available. Lean and low in fat, they make a healthy choice for a special occasion. Served with a sauce of fresh seasonal cranberries, port and ginger, they make a dish with a wonderful combination of flavors.

INGREDIENTS

Serves 4
1 orange
1 lemon
1 cup fresh or frozen
  cranberries
1 tsp grated fresh ginger
1 thyme sprig, plus extra to garnish
1 tsp Dijon mustard
4 tbsp red currant jelly
⅔ cup ruby port
2 tsp sunflower oil
4 venison steaks, 3½oz each
2 shallots, finely chopped
salt and black pepper
mashed potato and broccoli, to serve

NUTRITION NOTES

Per portion:
Energy	250Kcals/1055.5kJ
Fat	4.39g
Saturated fat	1.13g
Cholesterol	50mg
Fiber	1.59g

COOK'S TIP
When frying venison, always remember: the briefer the better. Venison will turn to leather if subjected to fierce heat after it has reached the medium-rare stage. If you dislike any hint of pink, cook it to this stage, then let it rest in a low oven for a few minutes.

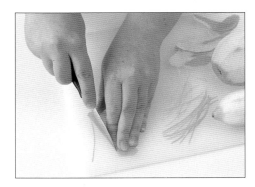

1 Pare the rind from half the orange and half the lemon using a vegetable peeler, then cut into very fine strips.

2 Blanch the strips in a small pan of boiling water for about 5 minutes, until tender. Drain the strips and refresh under cold water.

3 Squeeze the juice from the orange and lemon, then pour into a small pan. Add the cranberries, ginger, thyme sprig, mustard, red currant jelly and port. Cook over low heat until the jelly melts.

4 Bring the sauce to a boil, stirring occasionally, then cover the pan and reduce the heat. Cook gently for about 15 minutes, until the cranberries are just tender.

VARIATION
Substitute red currants for the cranberries. Stir them into the sauce toward the end of cooking with the orange and lemon rinds.

5 Heat the oil in a heavy frying pan, add the venison and cook over high heat for 2–3 minutes.

6 Turn over the steaks and add the shallots to the pan. Cook the steaks on the other side for 2–3 minutes, depending on whether you like rare or medium-cooked meat.

7 Just before the end of cooking, pour in the sauce and add the strips of orange and lemon rind.

8 Allow the sauce to bubble for a few seconds to thicken slightly, then remove the thyme sprig and adjust the seasoning to taste.

9 Transfer the venison steaks to warmed plates and spoon the sauce over them. Garnish with thyme sprigs and serve accompanied by mashed potato and broccoli.

WARM CHICKEN SALAD

Succulent cooked chicken pieces are combined with vegetables in a light chili dressing.

Serves 6

2oz mixed salad leaves
2oz baby spinach leaves
2oz watercress
2 tablespoons chili sauce
2 tablespoons dry sherry
1 tablespoon light soy sauce
1 tablespoon tomato ketchup
2 teaspoons olive oil
8 shallots, finely chopped
1 garlic clove, crushed
12oz skinless, boneless chicken breast,
    cut into thin strips
1 red bell pepper, seeded and sliced
6oz snow peas, trimmed
14oz can baby corn, drained and
    halved lengthwise
10oz can brown rice
salt and ground black pepper
fresh parsley sprig, to garnish

1 Arrange the mixed salad leaves, tearing up any large ones, and the spinach leaves on a serving dish. Add the watercress and toss to mix.

NUTRITION NOTES

Per portion:

Energy	190Kcals/801kJ
Fat	4.0g
Saturated Fat	0.91g
Cholesterol	25.1mg
Fiber	3.1g

2 In a small bowl, mix together the chili sauce, sherry, soy sauce and tomato ketchup and set aside.

3 Heat the oil in a large nonstick frying pan or wok. Add the shallots and garlic and stir-fry over a medium heat for 1 minute. Add the chicken and stir-fry for 3–4 minutes.

4 Add the bell pepper, snow peas, corn and rice and stir-fry for 2–3 minutes.

5 Pour in the chili sauce mixture and stir-fry for 2–3 minutes, until hot and bubbling. Season to taste. Spoon the chicken mixture over the salad leaves, toss together to mix and serve immediately, garnished with a fresh parsley sprig.

TANDOORI CHICKEN SKEWERS

This dish originates from the plains of the Punjab, at the foot of the Himalayas, where food is traditionally cooked in clay ovens known as tandoors – hence the name.

INGREDIENTS

Serves 4

4 boneless, skinless chicken breasts, about 3¹/₂oz each
1 tbsp lemon juice
3 tbsp tandoori paste
3 tbsp low fat plain yogurt
1 garlic clove, crushed
2 tbsp chopped cilantro
1 small onion, cut into wedges and separated into layers
1 tsp oil, for brushing
salt and black pepper
cilantro sprigs, to garnish
rice pilaf and nan, to serve

1 Chop the chicken breasts into 1in cubes, put in a bowl and add the lemon juice, tandoori paste, yogurt, garlic, cilantro and seasoning. Cover and let marinate in the fridge for 2–3 hours.

2 Preheat the broiler to high. Thread alternate pieces of chicken and onion onto four skewers.

COOK'S TIP
Use chopped, boned and skinned chicken thighs, or strips of turkey breasts, for a cheaper and equally low fat alternative.

3 Brush onions with a little oil, lay the skewers on a broiler rack and cook for 10–12 minutes, turning once.

4 Garnish the kebabs with cilantro and serve at once with rice pilaf and nan.

NUTRITION NOTES

Per portion:	
Energy	215.7Kcals/91.2kJ
Fat	4.2g
Saturated fat	0.27g
Cholesterol	122mg
Fiber	0.22g

SPAGHETTI BOLOGNESE

INGREDIENTS

Serves 8

1 onion, chopped
2–3 garlic cloves, crushed
1¼ cups beef or
 chicken stock
1 lb extra-lean ground turkey
 or beef
1 28oz can chopped tomatoes
1 tsp dried basil
1 tsp dried oregano
4 tbsp tomato paste
1 lb button mushrooms, quartered
 and sliced
⅔ cup red wine
1 lb spaghetti
salt and black pepper

NUTRITION NOTES

Per portion:

Energy	321Kcals/1350kJ
Fat	4.1g
Saturated fat	1.3g
Cholesterol	33mg
Fiber	2.7g

1 Put the chopped onion and garlic into a nonstick saucepan with half the stock. Bring to a boil and cook for 5 minutes, until the onion is tender and the stock has reduced completely.

COOK'S TIP
Sautéing vegetables in stock rather than oil is an easy way of saving calories and fat. Choose stock to reduce even more.

2 Add the turkey or beef and cook for 5 minutes, breaking up the meat with a fork. Add the tomatoes, herbs and tomato paste, bring to a boil, then cover and simmer for 1 hour.

3 Meanwhile, cook the mushrooms in a nonstick saucepan with the wine for 5 minutes or until the wine has evaporated. Add the mushrooms to the meat with salt and pepper to taste.

4 Cook the pasta in a large pan of boiling salted water for 8–12 minutes, until tender. Drain thoroughly. Serve topped with the meat sauce.

TURKEY AND PASTA BAKE

INGREDIENTS

Serves 4

10oz ground turkey
5oz smoked turkey bacon, chopped
1–2 garlic cloves, crushed
1 onion, finely chopped
2 carrots, diced
2 tbsp tomato paste
1¼ cups chicken stock
8oz rigatoni or penne pasta
2 tbsp grated Parmesan cheese
salt and black pepper

1 Brown the ground turkey in a non-stick saucepan, breaking up any large pieces with a wooden spoon, until well browned all over.

2 Add the chopped turkey bacon, garlic, onion, carrots, paste, stock and seasoning. Bring to a boil, cover and simmer for 1 hour, until tender.

3 Preheat the oven to 350°F. Cook the pasta in a large pot of boiling, salted water according to the package instructions, until *al dente*. Drain thoroughly and mix with the turkey sauce.

COOK'S TIP
Ground chicken or extra lean ground beef work just as well in this tasty recipe.

4 Transfer to a shallow ovenproof dish and sprinkle with grated Parmesan cheese. Bake for 20–30 minutes, until lightly browned on top.

NUTRITION NOTES

Per portion:

Energy	391Kcals/1641kJ
Fat	4.9g
Saturated fat	2.2g
Cholesterol	60mg
Fiber	3.5g

DUCK-BREAST SALAD

Tender slices of succulent cooked duck breasts served with a salad of mixed pasta, fruit and vegetables, tossed together in a light dressing, makes this a gourmet dish that will impress friends and family alike.

INGREDIENTS

Serves 6

2 small duck breasts, boned
1 tsp coriander, crushed
12oz rigatoni or penne pasta
⅔ cup fresh orange juice
1 tbsp lemon juice
2 tsp honey
1 shallot, finely chopped
1 garlic clove, crushed
1 celery stalk, chopped
3oz dried cherries
3 tbsp port
1 tbsp chopped fresh mint, plus extra to garnish
2 tbsp chopped cilantro, plus extra to garnish
1 eating apple, diced
2 oranges, segmented
salt and black pepper

COOK'S TIP
Choose skinless duck breasts to reduce both fat and calories. Crush your own whole spices, such as coriander seeds, to create fresh, aromatic, spicy flavors. Prepared ground spices lose their flavor more quickly than whole spices, which are best freshly ground just before use.

2 Cook the pasta in a large pot of boiling, salted water according to the package instructions, until *al dente*. Drain thoroughly and rinse under cold running water. Set aside to cool.

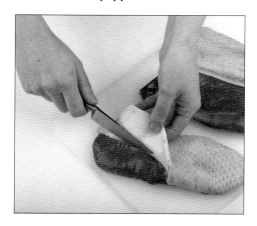

1 Remove the skin and fat from the duck breasts and season with salt and pepper. Rub with coriander seeds. Preheat the broiler, then broil the duck for 10 minutes on each side. Wrap in foil and let stand for 20 minutes.

3 To make the dressing, put the orange juice, lemon juice, honey, shallot, garlic, celery, cherries, port, mint and cilantro into a bowl, whisk together and allow to marinate for 30 minutes.

4 Slice the duck breasts very thinly. (They should be pink in the center.)

5 Put the pasta into a large bowl, then add the dressing, diced apple and segments of orange. Toss well to coat the pasta. Transfer the salad to a serving plate with the duck slices and garnish with the extra mint and cilantro.

NUTRITION NOTES

Per portion:	
Energy	348Kcals/1460kJ
Fat	3.8g
Saturated fat	0.9g
Cholesterol	55mg
Fiber	3g

FISH AND SEAFOOD

The range of fresh fish available in our supermarkets is impressive, and fish is always a good choice for a healthy low fat diet. Most fish, particularly white fish, is low in fat and is a good source of protein. Oily fish contains more fat than white fish, but contains high levels of essential fatty acids that are vital for good health. Fish is quick and easy to prepare and cook and is ideal for serving with fresh seasonal vegetables as part of a healthy low fat meal. Try Cajun-style Cod, Monkfish and Mussel Skewers or Curried Shrimp in Coconut Milk — just some of the delicious, low fat recipes included in this chapter.

CAJUN-STYLE COD

This recipe works equally well with any firm-fleshed fish – choose low fat fish, such as haddock or monkfish.

INGREDIENTS

Serves 4

4 cod steaks, about
  6oz each
2 tbsp low fat plain yogurt
1 tbsp lime or lemon juice
1 garlic clove, crushed
1 tsp ground cumin
1 tsp paprika
1 tsp mustard powder
½ tsp cayenne pepper
½ tsp dried thyme
½ tsp dried oregano
nonstick cooking spray
lemon slices, to garnish
new potatoes and a mixed green salad,
  to serve

NUTRITION NOTES

Per portion:

Energy	152Kcals/643kJ
Fat	1.9g
Saturated Fat	0.26g
Cholesterol	80.6mg
Fiber	0.1g

1 Pat the fish dry with paper towels. Combine the yogurt and lime or lemon juice and brush lightly over both sides of the fish.

2 Stir together the crushed garlic, spices and herbs. Coat both sides of the fish with the seasoning mix, rubbing in well.

3 Spray a ridged broiler pan or heavy frying pan with nonstick cooking spray. Heat until very hot. Add the fish and cook over high heat for 4 minutes, or until the undersides are well browned.

4 Turn the steaks over and cook for another 4 minutes or until cooked through. Serve immediately, garnished with lemon and accompanied by new potatoes and a mixed salad.

FLOUNDER PROVENÇAL

INGREDIENTS

Serves 4

4 large flounder fillets
2 small red onions
½ cup vegetable stock
4 tbsp dry red wine
1 garlic clove, crushed
2 zucchini, sliced
1 yellow bell pepper, seeded and sliced
1 14oz can chopped tomatoes
1 tbsp chopped fresh thyme
salt and black pepper
potato gratin, to serve

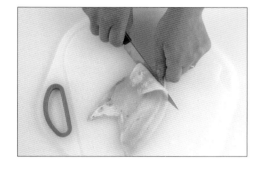

1 Preheat the oven to 350°F. If necessary, skin the fish: lay the flounder skin-side down and, holding the tail end, push a sharp knife between the skin and flesh in a sawing motion. Hold the knife at a slight angle with the blade towards the skin.

2 Cut each onion into eight wedges. Place in a heavy saucepan with the stock. Cover and simmer for 5 minutes. Uncover and continue to cook, stirring occasionally, until the stock has evaporated. Add the wine and garlic clove to the pan and continue to cook until the onions are soft.

3 Add the zucchini, yellow pepper, tomatoes and thyme and season to taste. Simmer for 3 minutes. Spoon the sauce into a large casserole.

> **COOK'S TIP**
> Skinless white fish fillets such as flounder or sand dab are low in fat and make an ideal tasty and nutritious basis for many low-fat recipes such as this one.

4 Fold each fillet in half and put on top of the sauce. Cover and cook in the oven for 15–20 minutes, until the fish is opaque and flakes easily. Serve with a potato gratin.

NUTRITION NOTES	
Per portion:	
Energy	195Kcals/822kJ
Fat	3.8g
Saturated Fat	0.61g
Cholesterol	63mg
Fiber	2.2g

MONKFISH AND MUSSEL SKEWERS

Skinless white fish such as monkfish is a good source of protein while also being low in calories and fat. These attractive seafood kebabs, flavored with a light marinade, are excellent broiled or barbecued and served with herbed boiled rice and a mixed green salad.

INGREDIENTS

Serves 4
1 lb monkfish, skinned and boned
1 tsp olive oil
2 tbsp lemon juice
1 tsp paprika
1 garlic clove, crushed
4 turkey bacon strips
8 cooked mussels
8 raw shrimp
1 tbsp chopped fresh dill
salt and black pepper
lemon wedges, to garnish
salad leaves and long-grain and wild
   rice, to serve

1 Cut the monkfish into 1in cubes and place in a shallow glass dish. Combine the oil, lemon juice, paprika and garlic. Season with pepper.

2 Pour the marinade over the fish and toss to coat evenly. Cover and put in a cool place for 30 minutes.

3 Cut the turkey bacon strips in half and wrap each strip around a mussel. Thread onto skewers, alternating with the fish cubes and raw shrimps. Preheat the broiler to high.

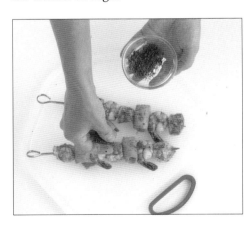

4 Broil the kebabs for 7–8 minutes, turning once and basting with the marinade. Sprinkle with chopped dill and salt. Garnish with lemon wedges and serve with salad and rice.

NUTRITION NOTES	
Per portion:	
Energy	145Kcals/604kJ
Fat	3.4g
Saturated Fat	0.81g
Cholesterol	84.7mg
Fiber	0.1g

BAKED COD WITH TOMATOES

For the very best flavor, use firm sun-ripened tomatoes for the sauce and make sure it is fairly thick before spooning it over the cod.

INGREDIENTS

Serves 4
2 tsp olive oil
1 onion, chopped
2 garlic cloves, finely chopped
1 lb tomatoes, peeled, seeded and chopped
1 tsp tomato paste
4 tbsp dry white wine
4 tbsp chopped flat leaf parsley
4 cod steaks
2 tbsp dried bread crumbs
salt and black pepper
new potatoes and green salad, to serve

NUTRITION NOTES

Per portion:
Energy	151Kcals/647kJ
Fat	1.5g
Saturated fat	0.2g
Cholesterol	55.2mg
Fiber	2.42g

COOK'S TIP
For extra speed, use a 14oz can of chopped tomatoes in place of the fresh tomatoes and 1–2 tsp prepared minced garlic in place of the garlic cloves.

1 Preheat the oven to 375°F. Heat the oil in a pan and fry the onion for about 5 minutes. Add the garlic, tomatoes, tomato paste, wine and seasoning.

2 Bring the sauce just to a boil, then reduce the heat slightly and cook, uncovered, for 15–20 minutes, until thick. Stir in the parsley.

3 Grease an ovenproof dish, put in the cod cutlets and spoon an equal amount of the tomato sauce onto each. Sprinkle the dried bread crumbs over the top.

4 Bake for 20–30 minutes, basting the fish occasionally with the sauce, until the fish is tender and cooked through, and the bread crumbs are golden and crisp. Serve hot with new potatoes and a green salad.

PINEAPPLE CURRY WITH SEAFOOD

The delicate sweet and sour flavor of this curry comes from the pineapple, and although it seems an odd combination, it is delicious.

INGREDIENTS

Serves 4
2½ cups coconut milk
2 tbsp red curry paste
2 tbsp fish sauce
1 tbsp sugar
8oz jumbo shrimp, shelled and
   deveined
1 lb mussels, cleaned and
   beards removed
6oz fresh pineapple, finely crushed
   or chopped
5 kafir lime leaves, torn
2 red chilies, chopped, and cilantro
   leaves, to garnish

1 In a large saucepan, bring half the coconut milk to a boil and heat, stirring, until it separates.

2 Add the red curry paste and cook until fragrant. Add the fish sauce and sugar and continue to cook for a few moments.

3 Stir in the rest of the coconut milk and bring back to a boil. Add the jumbo shrimp, mussels, pineapple and kafir lime leaves.

4 Reheat until boiling and then simmer for 3–5 minutes, until the shrimp are cooked and the mussels have opened. Remove any mussels that have not opened and discard. Serve garnished with chilies and cilantro.

NUTRITION NOTES	
Per portion:	
Energy	187Kcals/793kJ
Fat	3.5g
Saturated Fat	0.53g
Cholesterol	175.5mg
Fiber	0.59g

CURRIED SHRIMP IN COCONUT MILK

A curry-like dish where the shrimp are cooked in a spicy coconut gravy with sweet and sour flavors from the tomatoes.

INGREDIENTS

Serves 4
2½ cups coconut milk
2 tbsp Thai curry paste
1 tbsp fish sauce
½ tsp salt
1 tsp sugar
1 lb shelled jumbo shrimp, tails left
   intact and deveined
8oz cherry tomatoes
1 chili, seeded and chopped
juice of ½ lime, to serve
chili and cilantro, to garnish

1 Put half the coconut milk into a pan or wok and bring to a boil.

2 Add the curry paste to the coconut milk, stir until it disperses, then simmer for about 10 minutes.

3 Add the fish sauce, salt, sugar and remaining coconut milk. Simmer for another 5 minutes.

NUTRITION NOTES	
Per portion:	
Energy	184Kcals/778kJ
Fat	3.26g
Saturated fat	0.58g
Cholesterol	315mg
Fiber	0.6g

4 Add the shrimp, cherry tomatoes and chili. Simmer gently for about 5 minutes, or until the shrimp are pink and tender.

5 Serve sprinkled with lime juice and garnish with sliced chili and chopped cilantro leaves.

SHRIMP NOODLE SALAD

A light, refreshing salad with all the tangy flavor of the sea. Instead of shrimp, try squid, scallops, mussels or crab.

INGREDIENTS

Serves 4

4oz cellophane noodles, soaked in hot water until soft
16 cooked shrimp, peeled
1 small green bell pepper, seeded and cut into strips
½ cucumber, cut into strips
1 tomato, cut into strips
2 shallots, finely sliced
salt and black pepper
cilantro leaves, to garnish

For the dressing
1 tbsp rice vinegar
2 tbsp fish sauce
2 tbsp fresh lime juice
pinch of salt
½ tsp grated fresh ginger
1 lemongrass stalk, finely chopped
1 red chili, seeded and finely sliced
2 tbsp coarsely chopped mint
a few sprigs coarsely chopped tarragon
1 tbsp chopped chives

1 Make the dressing by combining all the ingredients in a small bowl or cup; whisk well.

2 Drain the noodles, then plunge them in a saucepan of boiling water for 1 minute. Drain, rinse under cold running water and drain again well.

3 In a large bowl, combine the noodles with the shrimp, pepper, cucumber, tomato and shallots. Lightly season with salt and pepper, then toss with the dressing.

4 Spoon the noodles onto individual plates. Garnish with a few cilantro leaves and serve at once.

NUTRITION NOTES

Per portion:

Energy	164.5Kcals/697kJ
Fat	2.9g
Saturated fat	0.79g
Cholesterol	121mg
Fiber	1.86g

COOK'S TIP
Shrimp are available ready-cooked and often shelled. To cook shrimp, boil them for 2 minutes. Allow them to cool in the cooking liquid, then gently pull off the tail shell and twist off the body.

PASTA WITH TOMATO AND TUNA

INGREDIENTS

Serves 6
1 medium onion, finely chopped
1 celery stalk, finely chopped
1 red bell pepper, seeded and diced
1 garlic clove, crushed
⅔ cup chicken stock
1 14oz can chopped tomatoes
1 tbsp tomato paste
2 tsp sugar
1 tbsp chopped fresh basil
1 tbsp chopped fresh parsley
1 lb pasta shells
1 14oz can tuna, drained
2 tbsp capers in vinegar, drained
salt and black pepper

1 Put the chopped onion, celery, red pepper and garlic into a nonstick pan. Add the stock, bring to a boil and cook for 5 minutes or until the stock has reduced almost completely.

2 Add the tomatoes, tomato paste, sugar and herbs. Season to taste and bring to a boil. Simmer for about 30 minutes, until thick, stirring occasionally.

3 Meanwhile, cook the pasta in a large pot of boiling, salted water according to the package instructions, until *al dente*. Drain thoroughly and transfer to a warm serving dish.

COOK'S TIP
If fresh herbs are not available, use a 14oz can of chopped tomatoes with herbs and add 1–2 tsp mixed dried herbs, in place of the fresh herbs.

4 Flake the tuna into large chunks and add to the sauce with the capers. Heat gently for 1–2 minutes, pour over the pasta, toss and serve immediately.

NUTRITION NOTES

Per portion:
Energy	369Kcals/1549kJ
Fat	2.1g
Saturated fat	0.4g
Cholesterol	34mg
Fiber	4g

VEGETABLES
AND SALADS

Vegetables, as an accompaniment or as a main course, provide a tasty and nutritious choice at mealtimes. There are a huge array of fresh vegetables from around the world available all year, so there's no excuse for not experimenting with new textures, colors and flavors. Choose from a wonderful selection of recipes, from delicious vegetarian main courses, such as Mixed Mushroom Ragoût, unusual side dishes like Zucchini and Asparagus Packages and Devilled Onions en Croûte, to light, flavorful salads, such as Marinated Cucumber Salad.

HERB BAKED TOMATOES

INGREDIENTS

Serves 4–6

1½ lb large red and yellow
   tomatoes
2 tsp red wine vinegar
½ tsp whole-grain mustard
1 garlic clove, crushed
2 tsp chopped fresh parsley
2 tsp chopped fresh chives
½ cup fresh fine white
   bread crumbs, for topping
salt and black pepper

NUTRITION NOTES

Per portion:
Energy	37Kcals/156kJ
Fat	0.49g
Saturated fat	0.16g
Cholesterol	0
Fiber	1.36g

1 Preheat the oven to 400°F. Thickly slice the tomatoes and arrange half of them in a 4 cup ovenproof casserole.

> **COOK'S TIP**
> Use whole-wheat bread crumbs in place of white, for added color, flavor and fiber. Use 1–2 tsp mixed dried herbs, if fresh herbs are not available.

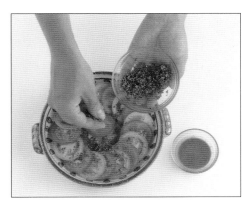

2 Mix the vinegar, mustard, garlic and seasoning together. Stir in 2 teaspoons cold water. Sprinkle the tomatoes with half the parsley and chives, then drizzle with half the dressing.

3 Lay the remaining tomato slices on top, overlapping them slightly. Drizzle with the remaining dressing.

4 Sprinkle with the bread crumbs. Bake for 25 minutes or until the topping is golden. Sprinkle with the remaining parsley and chives. Serve immediately, garnished with sprigs of parsley.

POTATO GRATIN

The flavor of Parmesan is wonderfully strong, so a little goes a long way. Leave the cheese out altogether for an almost fat-free dish.

─ INGREDIENTS ─

Serves 4
1 garlic clove
5 large baking potatoes, peeled
3 tbsp freshly grated Parmesan cheese
2½ cups vegetable or chicken stock
pinch of grated nutmeg
salt and black pepper

1 Preheat the oven to 400°F. Halve the garlic clove and rub the cut surface over the base and sides of a large shallow gratin dish.

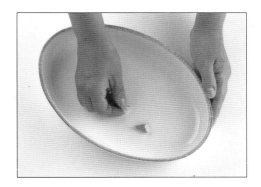

2 Slice the potatoes very thinly and arrange a third of them in the dish. Sprinkle with a little grated Parmesan cheese, and season with salt and pepper. Pour on some of the stock to prevent the potatoes from discoloring.

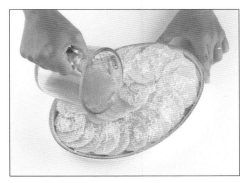

3 Continue layering the potatoes and cheese as before, then add the rest of the stock. Sprinkle with the grated nutmeg.

COOK'S TIP
For a potato and onion gratin, thinly slice one medium onion and layer with the potato.

4 Bake in the preheated oven for 1¼–1½ hours, or until the potatoes are tender and the tops well browned.

─ NUTRITION NOTES ─

Per portion:

Energy	190Kcals/802kJ
Fat	3.1g
Saturated Fat	1.60g
Cholesterol	7.5mg
Fiber	2.7g

DEVILED ONIONS EN CROÛTE

Fill crisp bread cups with tender button onions tossed in a mustard glaze. Try other low fat mixtures of vegetables, such as ratatouille, for a delicious change.

INGREDIENTS

Serves 4

*12 thin slices of white or
  whole-wheat bread
8oz button onions or shallots
1⅔ cup vegetable stock
1 tbsp dry white wine or
  dry sherry
2 turkey bacon strips, cut into thin strips
2 tsp Worcestershire sauce
1 tsp tomato paste
¼ tsp prepared mustard
salt and black pepper
sprigs of flat leaf parsley, to garnish*

1 Preheat the oven to 400°F. Cut the bread into rounds with a 3in fluted biscuit cutter and use to line a 12 cup muffin tin.

2 Cover each bread case with non-stick baking paper and fill with baking beans or weights. Bake for 5 minutes. Remove the paper and beans and bake for another 5 minutes, until lightly browned and crisp.

3 Meanwhile, put the button onions or shallots in a bowl and cover with boiling water. Let stand for 3 minutes, then drain and rinse under cold water. Trim off their top and root ends and slip them out of their skins.

4 Simmer the onions and stock in a covered saucepan for 5 minutes. Uncover and cook, stirring occasionally, until the stock has reduced entirely. Add all the remaining ingredients, except the flat leaf parsley, and cook for 2–3 minutes.

5 Fill the toast cups with the deviled onions. Serve hot, garnished with sprigs of flat leaf parsley.

NUTRITION NOTES	
Per portion:	
Energy	172Kcals/729kJ
Fat	1.5g
Saturated Fat	0.31g
Cholesterol	6.1mg
Fiber	1.7g

ZUCCHINI AND ASPARAGUS PACKAGES

To appreciate the aroma, these paper packages should be broken open at the table.

INGREDIENTS

Serves 4
2 medium zucchini
1 medium leek
8oz young asparagus, trimmed
4 tarragon sprigs
4 whole garlic cloves, unpeeled
1 egg, beaten, to glaze
salt and black pepper

NUTRITION NOTES

Per portion:	
Energy	52Kcals/215kJ
Fat	2.0g
Saturated Fat	0.43g
Cholesterol	48.1mg
Fiber	2.2g

1 Preheat the oven to 400°F. Using a potato peeler, carefully slice the zucchini lengthwise into thin strips.

2 Cut the leek into very fine julienne strips and cut the asparagus evenly into 2in lengths.

3 Cut out four sheets of parchment paper measuring 12 x 15 in and fold in half. Draw a large curve to make a heart shape when unfolded. Cut along the inside of the line and open out.

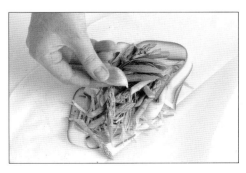

4 Divide the zucchini, asparagus and leek evenly between each paper heart, positioning the filling on one side of the fold line, and topping each with a sprig of tarragon and an unpeeled garlic clove. Season to taste.

5 Brush the edges lightly with the beaten egg and fold over.

6 Twist the edges together so that each package is completely sealed. Lay the packages on a baking sheet and cook for 10 minutes. Serve immediately.

COOK'S TIP
Experiment with other vegetable combinations, if desired.

MIXED MUSHROOM RAGOÛT

These mushrooms are delicious served hot or cold and can be prepared up to two days in advance.

INGREDIENTS

Serves 4
1 small onion, finely chopped
1 garlic clove, crushed
1 tbsp coriander seeds, crushed
2 tbsp red wine vinegar
1 tbsp soy sauce
1 tbsp dry sherry
2 tsp tomato paste
2 tsp light brown sugar
⅔ cup vegetable stock
4oz baby button mushrooms
4oz chestnut mushrooms, quartered
4oz oyster mushrooms, sliced
salt and black pepper
cilantro sprig, to garnish

NUTRITION NOTES

Per portion:
Energy	41Kcals/172kJ
Fat	0.7g
Saturated Fat	0.08g
Cholesterol	0
Fiber	1.0g

COOK'S TIP
There are many types of fresh mushrooms available and all are low in calories and fat. They add flavor and color to many low fat dishes such as this tasty ragoût.

1 Put the first nine ingredients in a large saucepan. Bring to a boil and reduce the heat. Cover and simmer for 5 minutes.

2 Uncover the saucepan and simmer for 5 more minutes, or until the liquid has reduced by half.

3 Add the baby button and chestnut mushrooms and simmer for 3 minutes. Stir in the oyster mushrooms and cook for another 2 minutes.

4 Remove the mushrooms from the pan with a slotted spoon and transfer them to a serving dish. Keep warm, if serving hot.

5 Boil the juices for about 5 minutes, or until reduced to about 5 tablespoons. Season to taste.

6 Allow to cool for 2–3 minutes, then pour on the mushrooms. Serve hot or well chilled, garnished with a sprig of cilantro.

Tofu and Green Bean Curry

This exotic curry is simple and quick to make. This recipe uses beans and mushrooms, but you can use almost any kind of vegetable, such as eggplant, bamboo shoots or broccoli.

INGREDIENTS

Serves 4
1½ cups coconut milk
1 tbsp red curry paste
3 tbsp fish sauce
2 tsp sugar
8oz button mushrooms
4oz green beans, trimmed
6oz tofu, rinsed and cut into
  ¾in cubes
4 kafir lime leaves, torn
2 red chilies, seeded and sliced
cilantro leaves, to garnish

NUTRITION NOTES

Per portion:	
Energy	100Kcals/420kJ
Fat	3.36g
Saturated fat	0.48g
Cholesterol	0
Fiber	1.35g

1 Put about one third of the coconut milk in a wok or saucepan. Cook until it starts to separate and an oily sheen appears.

2 Add the red curry paste, fish sauce and sugar to the coconut milk. Mix together thoroughly.

3 Add the mushrooms. Stir and cook for 1 minute.

4 Stir in the rest of the coconut milk and bring back to a boil.

> **COOK'S TIP**
> Use 1–2 tsp hot chili powder, if fresh red chilies aren't available. When preparing fresh chilies, wear rubber gloves and wash hands, work surfaces and utensils thoroughly afterwards. Chilies contain volatile oils which can irritate and burn sensitive areas, especially eyes.

5 Add the green beans and cubes of tofu and simmer gently for another 4–5 minutes.

6 Stir in the kafir lime leaves and chilies. Serve garnished with the cilantro leaves.

CACHUMBAR

Cachumbar is a salad relish most commonly served with Indian curries. There are many versions; this one will leave your mouth feeling cool and fresh after a spicy meal.

INGREDIENTS

Serves 4

3 ripe tomatoes
2 chopped scallions
¼ tsp sugar
salt
3 tbsp chopped fresh cilantro

NUTRITION NOTES

Per portion:

Energy	9.5Kcals/73.5kJ
Fat	0.23g
Saturated fat	0.07g
Cholesterol	0
Fiber	0.87g

1 Remove the tough cores from the bottom of the tomatoes with a small sharp-pointed knife.

COOK'S TIP
Cachumbar also makes a fine accompaniment to fresh crab, lobster and shellfish.

2 Halve the tomatoes, remove the seeds and dice the flesh.

3 Combine the tomatoes with the scallions, sugar, salt and chopped cilantro. Serve at room temperature.

MARINATED CUCUMBER SALAD

Sprinkling cucumbers with salt draws out some of the water and makes them softer and sweeter.

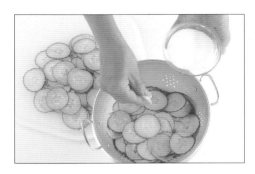

INGREDIENTS

Serves 6

2 medium cucumbers
1 tbsp salt
½ cup sugar
¾ cup dry cider
1 tbsp cider vinegar
3 tbsp chopped fresh dill
pinch of pepper

NUTRITION NOTES

Per portion:	
Energy	111Kcals/465kJ
Fat	0.1g
Saturated Fat	0.01g
Cholesterol	0
Fiber	0.62g

1 Slice the cucumbers thinly and place them in a colander, sprinkling salt between each layer. Put the colander over a bowl and set aside to drain for 1 hour.

COOK'S TIP
As a shortcut, leave out the method for salting cucumber described in step 1.

2 Thoroughly rinse the cucumber under cold running water to remove excess salt, then pat dry on absorbent paper towels.

3 Gently heat the sugar, cider and vinegar in a saucepan, until the sugar has dissolved. Remove from the heat and allow to cool. Put the cucumber slices in a bowl, pour the cider mixture over them and allow to marinate for about 2 hours.

4 Drain the cucumber and sprinkle with the dill and pepper to taste. Mix well and transfer to a serving dish. Chill in the fridge until ready to serve.

BULGUR AND MINT SALAD

INGREDIENTS

Serves 4

1⅔ cups bulgur
4 tomatoes
4 small zucchini, thinly sliced
    lengthwise
4 scallions, sliced on the diagonal
8 dried apricots, chopped
¼ cup raisins
juice of 1 lemon
2 tbsp tomato juice
3 tbsp chopped fresh mint
1 garlic clove, crushed
salt and black pepper
sprig of fresh mint, to garnish

1 Put the bulgur into a large bowl. Add enough boiling water to come 1in above the level of the wheat. Allow to soak for 30 minutes, then drain well and squeeze out any excess water in a clean dishtowel.

2 Meanwhile, plunge the tomatoes into boiling water for 1 minute and then into cold water. Slip off the skins. Halve, remove the seeds and cores and coarsely chop the flesh.

3 Stir the chopped tomatoes, zucchini, scallions, apricots and raisins into the bulgur.

4 Put the lemon and tomato juice, mint, garlic clove and seasoning into a small bowl and whisk together with a fork. Pour onto the salad and mix well. Chill for at least 1 hour. Serve garnished with a sprig of mint.

NUTRITION NOTES	
Per portion:	
Energy	297Kcals/1245kJ
Fat	1.7g
Saturated Fat	0.27g
Cholesterol	0
Fiber	2.4g

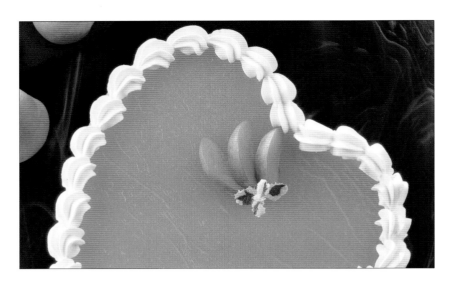

DESSERTS, CAKES AND BAKED GOODS

When we talk of desserts and cakes we tend to imagine deliciously rich, creamy, calorie-laden treats that are well out of reach for those who are following a low fat diet. However, with the right knowledge about low fat cooking methods it is very easy to create delicious, low fat desserts, cakes and baked goods that are also full of flavor and appeal. Try desserts such as Banana, Maple and Lime Crêpes and Strawberry and Apple Crisp, refreshing Iced Oranges and delicious cakes and baked goods, such as the classic Irish Whiskey Cake and Date and Apple Muffins.

STRAWBERRY AND APPLE CRISP

A high-fiber, healthier version of the classic apple crisp. Raspberries can be used instead of strawberries, either fresh or frozen.

INGREDIENTS

Serves 4

1 lb cooking apples
1¼ cups strawberries
2 tbsp sugar
½ tsp ground cinnamon
2 tbsp orange juice
yogurt, to serve

For the topping

3 tbsp plain whole-wheat flour
⅔ cup rolled oats
⅛ cup low fat margarine

1 Preheat the oven to 350°F. Peel, core and slice the apples. Halve the strawberries.

NUTRITION NOTES	
Per portion:	
Energy	182.3Kcals/785kJ
Fat	4g
Saturated fat	0.73g
Cholesterol	0.5mg
Fiber	3.87g

2 Toss together the apples, strawberries, sugar, cinnamon and orange juice. Pour into a 5 cup ovenproof dish, or four individual dishes.

3 Combine the flour and oats in a bowl and mix in the low fat margarine with a fork.

4 Sprinkle the topping evenly over the fruit. Bake for 40–45 minutes (20–25 minutes for individual dishes), until golden brown and bubbling. Serve warm with yogurt.

RAISIN AND COUSCOUS PUDDING

Most couscous on the market now is the pre-cooked variety, which needs only minimum cooking, but check the package instructions first to make sure. Serve hot, with yogurt or a low fat pudding.

INGREDIENTS

Serves 4
⅓ *cup golden raisins*
2 cups apple juice
1 cup couscous
½ *tsp pumpkin pie spice*

1 Lightly grease four 1 cup pudding molds or one 4 cup pudding mold. Put the raisins and apple juice in a pan.

2 Bring the apple juice to a boil, then cover the pan and let simmer gently for 2–3 minutes to plump up the fruit. Using a slotted spoon, lift out about half the fruit and put it in the bottom of the mold(s).

3 Add the couscous and pumpkin pie spice to the pan and bring back to a boil, stirring. Cover and leave over low heat for 8–10 minutes, or until the liquid has been absorbed.

NUTRITION NOTES	
Per portion:	
Energy	130.5Kcals/555kJ
Fat	0.40g
Saturated fat	0
Cholesterol	0
Fiber	0.25g

4 Spoon the couscous into the mold(s), spread it level, then cover the basin(s) tightly with foil. Put the mold(s) in a steamer over boiling water, cover and steam for about 30 minutes. Run a knife around the edges, turn the puddings out carefully and serve.

COOK'S TIP
As an alternative, use chopped dried apricots or pears in place of the raisins. Use unsweetened pineapple or orange juice in place of the apple juice.

BANANA MAPLE, AND LIME CRÊPES

Crêpes are a treat any day of the week, and they can be made in advance and stored in the freezer for convenience.

INGREDIENTS

Serves 4
1 cup flour
1 egg white
1 cup skim milk
¼ cup cold water
sunflower oil, for frying

For the filling
4 bananas, sliced
3 tbsp maple syrup
2 tbsp lime juice
strips of lime rind, to decorate

1 Beat together the flour, egg white, milk, and water until smooth and bubbly. Chill until needed.

2 Heat a small amount of oil in a nonstick frying pan and pour in enough batter just to coat the base. Swirl it around the pan to coat evenly.

3 Cook until golden, then toss or turn and cook the other side. Place on a plate, cover with foil, and keep hot while making the remaining crêpes.

4 To make the filling, place the bananas, syrup, and lime juice in a pan and simmer gently for 1 minute. Spoon into the crêpes and fold into quarters. Sprinkle with shreds of lime rind to decorate. Serve hot, with yogurt or low fat fromage frais.

> **COOK'S TIP**
> Crêpes freeze well. To store for later use, interleave them with nonstick baking paper, wrap, and freeze for up to 3 months.

NUTRITION NOTES	
Per portion:	
Energy	282Kcals/1185kJ
Fat	2.79g
Saturated fat	0.47g
Cholesterol	1.25mg
Fiber	2.12g

SPICED PEARS IN CIDER

Any variety of pear can be used for cooking, but it is best to choose firm pears for this recipe, or they will break up easily – Bosc are a good choice.

INGREDIENTS

Serves 4
4 medium firm pears
1 cup dry cider
thinly pared strip of lemon rind
1 cinnamon stick
2 tbsp brown sugar
1 tsp arrowroot
ground cinnamon, to sprinkle

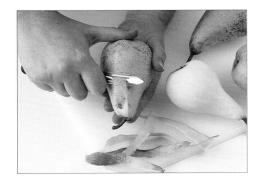

1 Peel the pears thinly, leaving them whole with the stems on. Place in a pan with the cider, lemon rind, and cinnamon. Cover and simmer gently, turning the pears occasionally for 15–20 minutes, or until tender.

2 Lift out the pears. Boil the syrup, uncovered, to reduce by about half. Remove the lemon rind and cinnamon stick, then stir in the sugar.

3 Mix the arrowroot with 1 tbsp cold water in a small bowl until smooth, then stir into the syrup. Bring to a boil and stir over the heat until thickened and clear.

4 Pour the sauce over the pears and sprinkle with ground cinnamon. Leave to cool slightly, then serve warm with low fat fromage frais.

COOK'S TIP
Whole pears look very impressive, but if you prefer, they can be halved and cored before cooking. This will reduce the cooking time slightly.

NUTRITION NOTES

Per portion:
Energy	102Kcals/428kJ
Fat	0.18g
Saturated fat	0.01g
Cholesterol	0
Fiber	1.65g

APRICOT DELICE

A fluffy mousse base with a
layer of fruit jelly on top makes
this dessert doubly delicious.

INGREDIENTS

Serves 8
*2 14oz cans apricots in
    natural juice*
4 tbsp sugar
5 tbsp lemon juice
5 tsp powdered gelatin
15 oz low fat ready-made pudding
²/₃ cup plain yogurt
*1 apricot, sliced, and fresh mint sprig,
    to decorate*
whipped cream, to decorate (optional)

NUTRITION NOTES

Per portion:
Energy	130Kcals/547kJ
Fat	1.9g
Saturated Fat	1.11g
Cholesterol	3.7mg
Fiber	0.7g

COOK'S TIP
Use low fat plain yogurt
to cut calories and fat. Add the
finely grated rind of 1 lemon
to the mixture, for extra flavor.
Peaches or pears are good
alternatives to apricots.

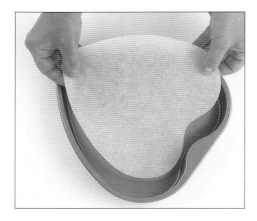

1 Line the base of a 5 cup heart-shaped or round cake tin with non-stick wax paper.

2 Drain the apricots, reserving the juice. Put the apricots in a food processor or blender fitted with a metal blade, together with the sugar and 4 tbsp of the apricot juice. Blend to a smooth purée.

3 Measure 2 tablespoons of the apricot juice into a small bowl. Add the lemon juice, then sprinkle on 2 tsp of the gelatin. Let stand for about 5 minutes, until spongy.

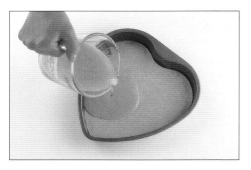

4 Stir the gelatin into half of the purée and pour into the prepared pan. Chill in the fridge for 1½ hours, or until firm.

5 Sprinkle the remaining 3 tsp of gelatin over 4 tbsp of the apricot juice. Let stand for about 5 minutes, until spongy. Mix the remaining apricot purée with the pudding, yogurt and gelatin. Pour onto the layer of set fruit purée and chill for 3 hours.

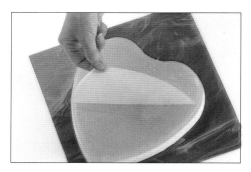

6 Dip the cake tin into hot water for a few seconds and unmold the delice onto a serving plate and peel off the lining paper. Decorate with the sliced apricot and mint sprig; for a special occasion, pipe whipped cream around the edge.

CRUNCHY FRUIT LAYER

INGREDIENTS

Serves 2

1 peach or nectarine
1 cup crunchy granola with nuts
⅔ cup low fat plain yogurt
1 tbsp jam
1 tbsp fruit juice

NUTRITION NOTES

Per portion:

Energy	227Kcals/950kJ
Fat	2.7g
Saturated Fat	0.98g
Cholesterol	3.0mg
Fiber	3.6g

1 Remove the pit from the peach or nectarine and cut the fruit into bite-size pieces with a sharp knife.

2 Divide the chopped fruit between two tall glasses, reserving a few pieces for decoration.

3 Sprinkle the granola over the fruit in an even layer, then top with the low fat yogurt.

4 Stir the jam and the fruit juice together in a cup, then drizzle the mixture over the yogurt. Decorate with the reserved peach or nectarine pieces and serve immediately.

ICED ORANGES

The ultimate fat-free treat – these delectable orange sherbets served in fruit shells were originally sold in beach cafés in the south of France.

INGREDIENTS

Serves 8
²⁄₃ cup sugar
juice of 1 lemon
14 medium oranges
8 fresh bay leaves, to decorate

NUTRITION NOTES

Per portion:
Energy	139Kcals/593kJ
Fat	0.17g
Saturated fat	0
Cholesterol	0
Fiber	3g

COOK'S TIP
Use crumpled paper towels to keep the shells upright.

1 Put the sugar in a heavy saucepan. Add half the lemon juice, then add ½ cup water. Cook over low heat until the sugar has dissolved. Bring to a boil and boil for 2–3 minutes, until the syrup is clear.

2 Slice the tops off eight of the oranges to make "hats." Scoop out the flesh of the oranges and reserve. Freeze the empty orange shells and "hats" until needed.

3 Grate the rind of the remaining oranges and add to the syrup. Squeeze the juice from the oranges, and from the reserved flesh. There should be 3 cups. Squeeze another orange or add bought orange juice, if necessary.

4 Stir the orange juice and remaining lemon juice, with 6 tablespoons water, into the syrup. Taste, adding more lemon juice or sugar as desired. Pour the mixture into a shallow freezer container and freeze for 3 hours.

5 Turn the orange sherbet mixture into a bowl and whisk thoroughly to break up the ice crystals. Freeze for 4 hours more, until firm, but not solid.

6 Pack the mixture into the hollowed-out orange shells, mounding it up, and set the "hats" on top. Freeze the sherbet shells until ready to serve. Just before serving, make a hole with a skewer in the tops of the "hats" and push in a bay leaf, to decorate.

IRISH WHISKEY CAKE

This moist rich fruit cake is drizzled with whiskey as soon as it comes out of the oven.

INGREDIENTS

Serves 12
⅔ cup candied cherries
1 cup dark brown sugar
⅔ cup golden raisins
⅔ cup dark raisins
½ cup currants
1¼ cups cold tea
2½ cups self-rising
   flour, sifted
1 egg
3 tbsp Irish whiskey

COOK'S TIP
If time is short, use hot tea and soak the fruit for just 2 hours.

1 Mix the cherries, sugar, dried fruit and tea in a large bowl. Allow to soak overnight until all the tea has been absorbed into the fruit.

NUTRITION NOTES

Per portion:	
Energy	265Kcals/1115kJ
Fat	0.88g
Saturated fat	0.25g
Cholesterol	16mg
Fiber	1.48g

2 Preheat the oven to 350°F. Grease and line a 2¼ lb loaf pan. Add the flour, then the egg to the fruit mixture and beat thoroughly until well mixed.

3 Pour the mixture into the prepared pan and bake for 1½ hours or until a skewer inserted into the center of the cake comes out clean.

4 Prick the top of the cake with a skewer and drizzle on the whiskey while the cake is still hot. Allow to stand for about 5 minutes, then remove from the pan and cool on a wire rack.

ANGEL CAKE

This cake makes a delicious light dessert, served on its own or with fresh fruit.

INGREDIENTS

Serves 10
⅓ *cup cornstarch*
⅓ *cup all-purpose flour*
8 egg whites
1 cup superfine sugar, plus extra for
  sprinkling
1 tsp vanilla extract
confectioners' sugar, for dusting

1 Preheat the oven to 350°F. Sift the flour and the cornstarch onto a sheet of wax paper.

2 Whisk the egg whites in a large, clean, dry bowl until very stiff, then gradually add the sugar and vanilla extract, whisking until the mixture is thick and glossy.

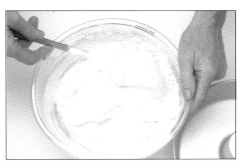

3 Gently fold in the flour mixture with a large metal spoon. Spoon into an ungreased 10-inch angel cake pan, smooth the surface and bake for about 45–50 minutes, or until the cake springs back when lightly pressed.

COOK'S TIP
Low fat cream cheese and fresh fruit are the ideal complement to this cake.

4 Sprinkle a piece of wax paper with sugar and set an egg cup in the center. Invert the cake pan over the paper, balancing it carefully on the egg cup. When cold, the cake will drop out of the tin. Transfer it to a plate, decorate, if desired, then dust with confectioners' sugar and serve.

NUTRITION NOTES	
Per portion:	
Energy	139Kcals/582kJ
Fat	0.08g
Saturated fat	0.01g
Cholesterol	0
Fiber	0.13g

COFFEE SPONGE DROPS

These are delicious on their own, but taste even better with a filling made by mixing low fat cream cheese with drained and chopped preserved ginger.

INGREDIENTS

Makes 12
$^{1}/_{2}$ cup all-purpose flour
1 tbsp instant
   coffee powder
2 eggs
6 tbsp superfine sugar

For the filling
$^{1}/_{2}$ cup low fat cream cheese
$^{1}/_{4}$ cup chopped preserved ginger

COOK'S TIP
As an alternative to preserved ginger in the filling, try walnuts.

1 Preheat the oven to 375°F. Line two baking sheets with nonstick parchment paper. Make the filling by beating together the cream cheese and preserved ginger. Chill until needed. Sift the flour and instant coffee powder together.

2 Combine the eggs and superfine sugar in a bowl. Beat with a hand-held electric whisk until thick and mousse-like. (When the whisk is lifted, a trail should remain on the surface of the mixture for at least 15 seconds.)

NUTRITION NOTES	
Per portion:	
Energy	69Kcals/290kJ
Fat	1.36g
Saturated fat	0.50g
Cholesterol	33.33mg
Fiber	0.29g

3 Carefully add the sifted flour and coffee mixture and gently fold in with a rubber spatula, being careful not to knock out any air.

4 Spoon the mixture into a pastry bag fitted with a $^{1}/_{2}$in plain nozzle. Pipe $1^{1}/_{2}$in rounds on the baking sheets. Bake for 12 minutes. Cool on a wire rack, then sandwich together with the filling.

DATE AND APPLE MUFFINS

You will only need one or two of these wholesome muffins per person, because they are very filling.

INGREDIENTS

Makes 12
1¼ cups self-rising whole-wheat flour
1¼ cups self-rising white flour
1 tsp ground cinnamon
1 tsp baking powder
2 tbsp soft margarine
½ cup light brown sugar
1 apple
1 cup apple juice
2 tbsp pear and apple spread
1 egg, lightly beaten
½ cup chopped dates
1 tbsp chopped pecans

1 Preheat the oven to 400°F. Arrange 12 paper cases in a deep muffin tin. Put the whole-wheat flour in a mixing bowl. Sift in the white flour with the cinnamon and baking powder. Rub in the margarine until the mixture resembles bread crumbs, then stir in the brown sugar.

NUTRITION NOTES

Per portion:
Energy	163Kcals/686kJ
Fat	2.98g
Saturated fat	0.47g
Cholesterol	16.04mg
Fiber	1.97g

2 Quarter and core the apple, chop the flesh finely and set aside. Stir a little of the apple juice with the pear and apple spread until smooth. Mix in the remaining juice, then add to the rubbed-in mixture with the egg. Add the chopped apple to the bowl with the dates. Mix quickly until just combined.

COOK'S TIP
Pear and apple spread is a highly concentrated paste. It is available in health food stores. You can substitute apple butter, but the flavor will not be as intense.

3 Divide the mixture among the muffin cases.

4 Sprinkle with the chopped pecans. Bake the muffins for 20–25 minutes, until golden brown and firm in the middle. Remove to a wire rack and serve while still warm.

PROSCIUTTO AND PARMESAN BREAD

This nourishing bread is almost a meal in itself.

INGREDIENTS

Serves 8
2 cups self-rising whole-wheat flour
2 cups self-rising white flour
1 tsp baking powder
1 tsp salt
1 tsp black pepper
3oz prosciutto
2 tbsp freshly grated Parmesan cheese
2 tbsp chopped fresh parsley
3 tbsp whole-grain mustard
1½ cups buttermilk
skim milk, to glaze

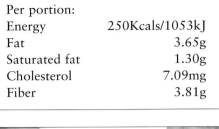

NUTRITION NOTES

Per portion:	
Energy	250Kcals/1053kJ
Fat	3.65g
Saturated fat	1.30g
Cholesterol	7.09mg
Fiber	3.81g

1 Preheat the oven to 400°F. Flour a baking sheet. Place the whole-wheat flour in a bowl and sift in the white flour, baking powder and salt. Add the pepper and the ham. Set aside about 1 tbsp of the grated Parmesan and stir the rest into the flour mixture with the parsley. Make a well in the center.

2 Mix the mustard and buttermilk, pour into the flour and quickly mix to a soft dough.

3 Turn the dough onto a floured surface and knead briefly. Shape into an oval loaf, brush with milk and sprinkle with the Parmesan cheese. Put the loaf on the prepared baking sheet.

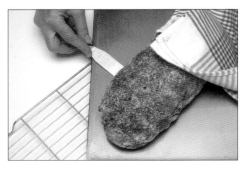

4 Bake the loaf for 25–30 minutes. Allow to cool before serving.

PEAR AND RAISIN QUICK BREAD

This is an ideal quick bread to make when pears are plentiful – an excellent use for windfalls.

INGREDIENTS

Serves 6–8
¼ *cup rolled oats*
¼ *cup light brown sugar*
2 *tbsp pear or apple juice*
2 *tbsp sunflower oil*
1 *large or 2 small pears*
1 *cup self-rising flour*
¾ *cup raisins*
½ *tsp baking powder*
2 *tsp pumpkin pie spice*
1 *egg*

1 Preheat the oven to 350°F. Grease and line a 1 lb loaf tin with non-stick parchment paper. Put the oats in a bowl with the sugar, pour over the pear or apple juice and oil, mix well and allow to stand for 15 minutes.

2 Quarter, core and coarsely grate the pear(s). Add to the oat mixture with the flour, raisins, baking powder, pumpkin pie spice and egg, then combine thoroughly.

3 Spoon the mixture into the prepared loaf pan and level the top. Bake for 50–60 minutes or until a skewer inserted into the center comes out clean.

> COOK'S TIP
> Health food shops sell concentrated pear and apple juice, ready for diluting as needed.

4 Transfer the quick bread onto a wire rack and peel off the lining paper. Allow to cool completely.

NUTRITION NOTES

Per portion:
Energy	200Kcals/814kJ
Fat	4.61g
Saturated fat	0.79g
Cholesterol	27.50mg
Fiber	1.39g

INDEX